The Best of

COOKING
with
SHOTGUN RED.

VOLUME 2

Is this the BEST Cookbook?
If it ain't...
It ought to be!

Jennifer Bruce and Miss Sheila Keeton

SGR
PUBLISHING

Editor: Donna Wilms
Recipe photography by Jennifer Bruce and Miss Sheila Keeton
Cover and design by Jennifer Bruce

www.Shotgunred.com

CONTENTS

Preface and Dedication

Steve Hall and Shotgun Red
Dec 1, 1954 - Dec 29, 2018

The popular YouTube Channel, "Cooking with Shotgun Red", was created by television personality, entertainer, musician, comedian, and creator of the world-famous Shotgun Red character, Steve Hall. Steve opened every show with his famous quote, "Hunter, fisher, trapper, trader, guide, scout, interpreter, and just a country cook, Steve Hall", and closed every show with, "Is this the best? If it ain't... it ought to be!". Before Steve Hall passed away in December 2018, he had uploaded 307 recipes to the Cooking with Shotgun Red channel. Since his passing, people around the world are still discovering all of these great recipes as Cooking with Shotgun Red continues to grow each year.

Miss Sheila, Steve's Fiancé and co-host, and long time friend and Shotgun Red Band mate, Jennifer Bruce, continue to carry on his legacy sharing new recipes, entertaining folks, and sharing Steve's love of cooking. Steve started a cookbook before he passed, but never had an opportunity to complete it. Miss Sheila and Jennifer decided to finish the cookbook, and now they have completed a second cookbook, "The Best of Cooking with Shotgun Red" recipes! He would be so proud!

Jennifer Bruce and Miss Sheila
"Two Forks Up"

You can find out more by visiting
www.Shotgunred.com

SUBSTITUTIONS LIST

INGREDIENT	AMOUNT	SUBSTITUTION
Allspice	1 teaspoon	1/2 tsp cinnamon, 1/4 tsp ginger, and 1/4 tsp cloves
Baking powder	1 teaspoon	1/4 tsp baking soda + 1/2 tsp cream of tartar OR 1/4 tsp baking soda + 1/2 cup buttermilk (decrease liquid in recipe by 1/2 cup)
Beer	1 cup	1 cup nonalcoholic beer OR 1 cup chicken broth
Bread crumbs	1 cup	1 cup cracker crumbs OR 1 cup matzo meal OR 1 cup ground oats
Broth (beef or chicken)	1 cup	1 bouillon cube + 1 cup boiling water OR 1 tbls soy sauce + enough water to make1 cup OR 1 cup vegetable broth
Brown sugar	1 cup packed	1 cup white sugar + 1/4 cup molasses & decrease the liquid in recipe by 1/4 cup OR 1 cup white sugar
Butter	1 cup	1 cup shortening OR 7/8 cup vegetable oil OR 7/8 cup lard
Chervil	1 tbsp chopped fresh	1 tbsp chopped fresh parsley
Chicken base	1 tablespoon	1 cup canned or homemade chicken broth or stock. Reduce liquid in recipe by 1 cup
Corn syrup	1 cup	1 1/4 cup white sugar plus 1/3 cup water OR 1 cup honey OR 1 cup light treacle syrup
Cottage cheese	1 cup	1 cup farmer's cheese OR 1 cup ricotta cheese
Cream (half and half)	1 cup	7/8 cup milk plus 1 tbsp butter
Cream (heavy)	1 cup	1 cup evaporated milk OR 3/4 cup milk + 1/3 cup butter
Cream (light)	1 cup	1 cup evaporated milk OR 3/4 cup milk plus 3 tbsp butter
Cream (whipped)	1 cup	1 cup frozen whipped topping, thawed
Cream cheese	1 cup	1 cup pureed cottage cheese OR 1 cup plain yogurt, strained overnight in a cheesecloth
Cream of tartar	1 teaspoon	2 tsp lemon juice or vinegar
Egg	1 whole	2 1/2 tbsp of powdered egg substitute + 2 1/2 tbsp water OR 1/4 cup liquid egg substitute OR 1/4 cup silken tofu pureed OR 3 tbsp mayonnaise OR half a banana mashed with 1/2 tsp baking powder OR 1 tbsp powdered flax seed soaked in 3 tbsp water
Evaporated milk	1 cup	1 cup light cream
Fats for baking	1 cup	1 cup applesauce OR 1 cup fruit puree
Flour (Bread Flour)	1 cup	1 cup all-purpose flour + 1 tsp wheat gluten
Flour (Cake Flour)	1 cup	1 cup all-purpose flour minus 2 tbsp
Flour (Self-Rising)	1 cup	7/8 cup all-purpose flour + 1 1/2 tsp baking powder & 1/2 tsp of salt
Garlic	1 clove	1/8 tsp garlic powder OR 1/2 tsp granulated garlic OR 1/2 tsp garlic salt (reduce salt in recipe)
Gelatin	1 tbsp	granulated 2 teaspoons agar agar
Green onion	1 cup chopped	1 cup chopped onion, OR 1 cup chopped leek OR 1 cup chopped shallots
Hazelnuts	1 cup whole	1 cup macadamia nuts OR 1 cup almonds
Honey	1 cup	1 1/4 cup white sugar + 1/3 cup water OR 1 cup corn syrup OR 1 cup light treacle syrup

KITCHEN CONVERSIONS

TEASPOON	TABLESPOON	CUPS	MILLILITERS	FLUID OUNCES
1 tsp	1/3 tbsp	1/48 cup	5 ml	1/8 oz
3 tsp	1 tbsp	1/16 cup	15 ml	1/2 oz
6 tsp	2 tbsp	1/8 cup	30 ml	1 oz
12 tsp	4 tbsp	1/4 cup	59 ml	2 oz
16 tsp	5 1/3 tbsp	1/3 cup	79 ml	2 2/3 oz
24 tsp	8 tbsp	1/2 cup	118 ml	4 oz
32 tsp	10 2/3 tbsp	2/3 cup	158 ml	5 1/3 oz
36 tsp	12 tbsp	3/4 cup	177 ml	6 oz
48 tsp	16 tbsp	1 cup	237 ml	8 oz

FAHRENHEIT	CELSIUS
275 F	140 C
300 F	150 C
325 F	165 C
350 F	177 C
375 F	190 C
400 F	200 C
425 F	220 C
450 F	230 C
475 F	245 C
500 F	260 C

MEAT TEMPERATURE GUIDE	
Beef	@ 140 = rare @ 160 = medium @ 170 = well done
Pork	ground @ 160 = safe roast @ 165 = safe
Whole Chicken	@ 180 = safe
Whole Turkey	@ 180 = safe
Lamb Roast	@ 145 = safe

a pinch = 1/8 teaspoon

3 teaspoon = 1 tablespoon

4 tablespoons = 1 cup

2 cups = 1 pint

2 pints = 1 quart

4 quarts = 1 gallon

8 quarts = 1 peck

4 pecks = 1 bushel

APPETIZERS

BACON WRAPPED JALAPEÑO POPPERS

INGREDIENTS:

- 6 Large jalapeño Peppers
- 1 8oz. Box Cream Cheese (softened)
- ½ Cup Shredded Monterey Jack Cheese
- ½ Cup Cilantro (finely chopped)
- 1 1 lb. Package Thin Sliced Smoked Bacon
- Sazon All Purpose Seasoning

Prep. time:
10 min

Total time:
45 min

Serves: 6

Enjoy and serve with ranch dressing. It's great dipping sauce and you can spice it up by adding a little sriracha sauce.

DIRECTIONS:

1. Preheat oven or grill to 350 degrees.

2. Slice each jalapeño pepper in half lengthwise and clean out the seeds and white ribs with a spoon.

3. In a bowl, mix together the softened cream cheese, shredded Monterey jack cheese, and finely chopped cilantro. Fill each jalapeño pepper half with the cream cheese mixture. Sprinkle lightly with sazon all purpose seasoning. Then wrap each jalapeño half with a slice of bacon starting with the big end of the pepper.

4. Place the peppers on a baking sheet lined with foil and sprayed with nonstick cooking spray. Bake in the oven uncovered at 350 degrees for about 45 minutes, or until the bacon is brown and crispy. You can also place them directly on the grill. (If you are using the grill, spray the grill grate with nonstick cooking spray and make sure only one side has coals or burners on and cook the peppers on the other side of the grill covered.)

DEEP FRIED DILL PICKLE ON A STICK

INGREDIENTS:

- 4 Large Dill Pickles
- 1½ Cups Buttermilk
- 1 Cup All-Purpose Flour
- 1 Tbsp. Baking Soda
- 1 Tbsp. Paprika
- ½ Tsp. Salt
- ½ Tsp. Pepper
- 1 Egg (beaten)
- 2 Cups Cool Ranch Tortilla Chips (finely crushed)
- Vegetable Oil for frying
- Bamboo Skewers
- Ranch Dressing for dipping sauce

"Sheila likes to call these Picklesicles"
Steve Hall

Prep. time:
15 min

Total time:
3 min

Serves: 4

DIRECTIONS:

1. Cut off the vine end of each dill pickle. Then stick a skewer full length through the center. Using a sharp knife, cut the pickle starting at the top on an angle all the way to the bottom into a spiral.
2. In a bowl, add the buttermilk, flour, baking soda, paprika, salt, pepper and egg. Whisk together until all ingredients are well combined and the batter is smooth.
3. In a shallow pan, add the finely crushed tortilla chips. Then pour the batter mixture into another shallow pan. Dip each pickle into the batter mixture and then place into the pan with the crushed tortilla chips. Press the tortilla chips on the pickle so it is completely coated.
4. In a deep fry pan, add vegetable oil and heat to 350 degrees. Then deep fry each pickle for 2 to 3 minutes, or until tortilla chips are golden brown and crispy. Place on a plate lined with paper towels. Drizzle with ranch dressing and serve.

SWEET ONION DIP

INGREDIENTS:

- 2 Cups Sweet Onions (finely diced)
- 1½ Cups Sharp Cheddar Cheese (shredded)
- 8 Slices American Cheese (cut into quarters)
- ¾ Cup Mayonnaise
- 4 Tbsp. Green Onions (chopped/ divided)

"Sweet onions are so delicious…. I can pick one up and take a big bite out of it just like an apple" Steve Hall

Prep. time: 10 min | Total time: 25 min | Serves: 6-8

DIRECTIONS:

1. Preheat oven to 375 degrees.

2. In a large bowl, add onions, cheddar cheese, American cheese, mayonnaise, and 2 tbsp. green onions. Mix together until well combined.

3. Spoon the mixture into a lightly greased 1 quart baking dish. Then place in the oven and bake for 25 minutes, or until golden brown and bubbly.

4. Remove from the oven and garnish with chopped green onions. Serve warm with butter crackers, chips, or slices of crusty bread.

GOLDEN BROWN ASPARAGUS FRIES

Prep. time: 15 min | Total time: 5 min | Serves: 6-8

INGREDIENTS:

- 1 Bundle Asparagus (medium thickness)
- ½ Cup Sour Cream
- 1 Tbsp. Lemon Juice
- 1 Tbsp. Dijon Mustard
- 1 Tsp. Sugar
- ¼ Tsp. Salt
- ½ Tsp. Pepper
- 1 Cup All-Purpose Flour
- 4 Eggs (beaten)
- 2 Cups Seasoned Breadcrumbs
- Vegetable Oil

DIRECTIONS:

1. Snap off the bottom (about 1 - 2 inches) of the asparagus stems using your fingers, or cut off with a knife. Rinse well with cool water, then place in a bowl of water and set aside.
2. In a deep fry pan, add vegetable oil (about 2 inches deep) and heat to 300 - 325 degrees.
3. While the oil is heating up, make the dipping sauce. In a bowl mix together sour cream, lemon juice, Dijon mustard, sugar, salt, and pepper. Then set aside.
4. Set out 3 shallow pans or bowls. In bowl #1 add all-purpose flour. In bowl #2 add eggs. In bowl #3 add seasoned breadcrumbs.
5. Shake excess water off each asparagus spear and dredge in flour, then dip in egg wash, and then roll in the seasoned breadcrumbs.
6. Drop each spear gently into the hot oil and fry until golden brown (about 2 minutes). Then place on a plate lined with paper towels. Serve with the special dipping sauce and enjoy!

PEANUT BUTTER AND JELLY WINGS

Prep. time:
10 min

Total time:
15 min

Serves: 2

INGREDIENTS:

- 1 3 lb. Package Chicken Wings
- ½ Cup Cornstarch
- ½ Cup Water
- Vegetable Oil for frying
- 1 Cup Peanut Butter
- 1 Cup Grape Jelly
- 1 Tbsp. Soy Sauce
- 1 Tbsp. Sriracha Sauce
- ¾ Cup Orange Juice
- ½ Cup Pecans
  (finely chopped / divided)
- Chopped Green Onions for garnish

DIRECTIONS:

1. In a bowl, add cornstarch and water and whisk together until smooth to make a slurry. Then add the chicken wings into the bowl and coat well with the slurry.

2. In a deep fry pan, add vegetable oil (about 2 inches deep) and heat to 350 degrees. Fry chicken wings in batches about 9 - 10 minutes, or until golden brown (do not overcrowd the fry pan when frying each batch). Remove the wings and place them on a plate lined with paper towels.

3. In a saucepan, add peanut butter, grape jelly, soy sauce, sriracha sauce, and orange juice, and stir together until creamy. Then add 1 tbsp. chopped pecans and reserve the remainder for garnish). On medium-low heat, simmer for 5 minutes (stirring occasionally).

4. Place wings in the saucepan with the peanut butter sauce and continue to simmer for another 2 minutes. Transfer wings to a serving platter and sprinkle with the chopped pecans and green onions. Wait until you taste these.....they are so delicious!

BREAKFAST

LOADED BREAKFAST SKILLET HASH

INGREDIENTS:

- 1 Bag Potatoes O'Brien (thawed)
- 6 Slices Thick Bacon (chopped)
- 1 Cup Fully Cooked Breakfast Sausage (chopped)
- 1 Cup Fully Cooked Ham (chopped)
- ½ Cup Red Onion (diced)
- 1 Cup Mushrooms (quartered)
- 2 Tbsp. Olive Oil
- 4 Eggs
- ¼ Cup Green Onions (chopped)
- ½ Cup Shredded Cheese Blend
- Salt and Pepper

Prep. time:
15 min

Total time:
30 min

Serves: 4

DIRECTIONS:

1. Preheat oven 400 degrees.

2. In a cast iron skillet on medium heat add olive oil, then add bacon and cook until almost crispy. Transfer the bacon using a slotted spoon to a plate lined with paper towels, and set aside.

3. Add sausage and ham into the bacon drippings in the skillet and cook on medium heat for about 1 minute, then transfer them to the plate with the bacon using a slotted spoon and set aside. Add red onions and mushrooms to the bacon drippings in the skillet and sauté until onions are soft and the mushrooms reduce.

4. Then add the thawed potatoes into the skillet with the red onions and mushrooms. Partially cover and cook the potatoes for about 5 minutes. Remove the cover and cook on medium-high heat (flipping the potatoes every few minutes) until potatoes are brown and crispy. Then stir in the cooked bacon, ham and sausage.

5. Using a large ladle or spoon, make four wells in the hash mixture. Then crack an egg into each of the four wells.

6. Top with shredded cheese, green onions, and season with salt, and pepper. Bake in the oven for about 15 minutes, or until the eggs are cooked to your liking, the hash is golden brown, and the cheese has melted. Serve and enjoy!

FRIED SHREDDED WHEAT

INGREDIENTS:

- 4 Shredded Wheat Big Biscuits
- 1 Cup Half & Half or Milk
- 4 Tbsp. Butter
- 4 Tsp. Sugar

"My mom made this for me when I was a kid, and it's still my favorite for breakfast"
Steve Hall

DIRECTIONS:

Prep. time: 5 min | Total time: 10 min | Serves: 2

1. Pour the half & half or milk into a microwave safe bowl. Warm it in the microwave on medium-high heat for 30 - 60 seconds. Check and stir every 15 seconds and remove when steam begins to rise.
2. In a large frying pan on medium heat, melt butter. Dip each shredded wheat biscuit in the bowl with warm half & half or milk. Then slightly drain each biscuit and place in the frying pan. Fry both sides until golden brown (use a spatula to press down each biscuit while frying). Serve in a bowl of warm half & half or milk and sprinkle with sugar and enjoy!

CHIPPED BEEF GRAVY ON TOAST aka S.O.S.

INGREDIENTS:

- 1 5oz. Jar Sliced Dried Beef
- 8 Tbsp. Butter
- 8 Tbsp. All-Purpose Flour
- 4 Cups Whole Milk
- Salt and Pepper
- 8 Slices of Bread (your choice / toasted)

DIRECTIONS:

Prep. time: 10 min | Total time: 10 min | Serves: 2-4

1. Chop the sliced dried beef into bite-sized pieces and set aside.
2. In a skillet on medium heat, add butter. Once the butter has melted, whisk in the flour and cook for 2 to 3 minutes, whisking continuously. Then slowly pour milk into the skillet a little at a time. Bring to a simmer and continue to whisk for about 5 minutes, or until the gravy has thickened and is smooth and creamy.
3. Add the dried beef into the skillet with the gravy, stir and let simmer for a few more minutes. Season with salt and pepper to taste.
4. Serve hot on top of toasted bread slices. It's delicious over biscuits too!

STEVE'S BREAKFAST FLAT WRAPS

INGREDIENTS:

- 6 Large Flour Tortillas (taco size)
- 1 Tsp. Vegetable or Olive Oil
- 6 Tbsp. Butter (divided)
- 1 16oz. Pkg. Smoked Sausage (cut into bite-sized pieces)
- ½ Cup Sweet Onions (diced)
- ½ Cup Green Peppers (diced)
- ½ Cup Mushrooms (quartered)
- 12 Eggs
- ½ Tsp. Salt
- ½ Tsp. Pepper
- ¼ Cup Mayonnaise
- 1 Cup Shredded Cheese (your choice)
- 2 Tomatoes (diced)
- Garnish with Sour Cream and Salsa

Prep. time:
10 min

Total time:
20 min

Serves: 6

DIRECTIONS:

1. In a large nonstick skillet on medium heat, add oil and 3 tbsp. butter. Once the butter has melted, add the smoked sausage, onions, peppers, and mushrooms and cook until the veggies are tender.

2. Add the eggs into the skillet with the sausage and veggies. Using a spatula, stir continuously until the eggs are scrambled and cooked until firm, or to desired doneness. Season with salt and pepper.

3. Place each tortilla on a clean flat surface and spread some mayonnaise on each tortilla. Then spoon some of the eggs, sausage, and veggies down the center of each tortilla, and sprinkle with shredded cheese and some diced tomatoes. Fold the tortilla in half, then roll up and press down to make a flat wrap.

4. Melt 3 tbsp. butter in a nonstick skillet on medium heat. Place each flat wrap in the skillet and cook on both sides until golden brown. Serve with sour cream and salsa and enjoy!

FANCY FRENCH TOAST

INGREDIENTS:

- 4 Slices Texas Toast Bread
- 5 Eggs
- ½ Cup Half & Half
- ½ Tbsp. Brown Sugar
- 1 Tsp. Vanilla
- ½ Tsp. Cinnamon
- 1 Stick Butter (divided)
- 1 Tbsp. Vegetable Oil

Toppings:
- Powdered Sugar
- Pure Maple Syrup
- Fresh Fruit (your choice)

Prep. time:
10 min

Total time:
10 min

Serves: 2

DIRECTIONS:

1. In a bowl, whisk together the eggs, half & half, brown sugar, vanilla, and cinnamon. Then pour the egg mixture into a shallow dish.

2. In a microwave safe bowl, melt 4 tbsp. butter, then stir in 1 tbsp. vegetable oil. Pour and spread the butter mixture evenly with a spatula onto a griddle set on medium heat.

3. Dip each slice of bread into the egg mixture and let soak about 10 seconds per side. Then place on the hot griddle and fry until golden brown on both sides. Put a pat of butter on top of each slice of French toast.

4. Place the French toast on a serving plate with a generous sprinkle of powdered sugar and drizzle with some warm pure maple syrup…..fresh fruit is also delicious on top!

"The key to the best French toast is powdered sugar on top" Steve Hall

HOMEMADE VENISON OR PORK SAUSAGE

INGREDIENTS:

- 3 lbs. Venison or Pork Butt (cubed)
- 2 lbs. Pork Butt (cubed)
- 12oz. Hickory Smoked Bacon

Seasoning Mixture:
- 3 Tbsp. Brown Sugar
- 4 Tsp. Rubbed Sage
- 4 Tsp. Black Pepper
- 4 Tsp. Kosher Salt
- 3 Tsp. Parsley Flakes
- 1 Tsp. Garlic Powder
- 1 Tsp. Thyme (or a bit more)
- 1 Tsp. Rosemary
- 2 Tsp. Red Pepper Flakes
- ½ Tsp. Ground Nutmeg
- ¼ Tsp. Dried Marjoram
- ½ Tsp. Orange Zest
- (or a bit more)
- 1 Tsp. Lightly Chopped
- Fennel Seed

Total time:
24 Hours

DIRECTIONS:

1. Place the venison, pork, and bacon in the freezer for about 30 minutes, or until very cold, or partially frozen. Remove from the freezer and grind the cold cubes of meat using a course plate on the grinder. Mix the ground meats together in a large bowl, then cover the bowl with plastic wrap and put it in the refrigerator while preparing the seasoning mixture.

2. In a separate bowl, pour in 6 oz. of cold water, add all the seasoning mixture ingredients, and whisk together well.

3. Then take the sausage mixture out of the refrigerator, pour the seasoning mixture over the sausage and mix in well. Cover the bowl of sausage with plastic wrap and put it in the refrigerator overnight.

4. The next day, take the sausage out of the refrigerator and run it through the grinder one more time (see important note below). Then form into breakfast sausage patties, or stuff casings for breakfast sausage links.

5. This is a fresh sausage, so you can not cold smoke it. It must be refrigerated at all times and cooked within 2 to 3 days, or you can keep it uncooked in the freezer for 2 to 3 months.

Note: Important! After you mix the seasoning in the sausage and refrigerate it overnight, run the last grind through a real coarse plate so that the sausage mixture stays moist. A fine plate is okay if you are stuffing links, but using a coarse plate for patties will give them a better texture and flavor. Make sure the meat stays cold and place it in the refrigerator while preparing the seasoning mixture, or stuffing casings and making the patties.

BUNS, BREAD AND ROLLS

SWEET DINNER ROLLS

INGREDIENTS:

- 2 Packets Active Dry Yeast (1 packet = 2 ¼ tsp.)
- ¾ Cup Lukewarm Water or Milk
- 1 Tsp. Sugar (to activate yeast)
- 5 Tbsp. Sugar (add to dry ingredients)
- 4 – 5 Cups All-Purpose Flour
- 1 Tsp. Salt
- 1 Large Egg (room temperature)
- ½ Cup Unsweetened Pineapple Juice (room temperature)
- 1½ Sticks Butter (melted and slightly cooled - divided)
- Vegetable Oil

Prep. time: 90 min

Total time: 30 min

Serves: 6

DIRECTIONS:

1. Heat oven to 150 degrees, then turn the heat off. Pour hot water into a pan and place on the bottom rack in the oven.

2. In a glass measuring cup, add water and warm it in the microwave until the temperature is between 98 and 110 degrees. Then add 1 tsp. sugar and the active dry yeast, and stir gently until dissolved. Set aside for 8 to 10 minutes until the yeast activates and has bubbled and looks frothy on top of the water.

DIRECTIONS CONTINUED:

3. In the bowl of a stand mixer, add 4 cups flour, 5 tbsp. sugar, and salt. Mix together using the paddle attachment on low speed for about 1 minute. Then add the egg, pineapple juice, 5 tbsp. melted butter (reserve the rest to baste rolls), and water/yeast mixture, and mix together until combined. Remove the paddle attachment and replace with a dough hook. Kneed on medium-low speed and gradually add in ½ to 1 more cup of flour until the dough forms into a soft ball.

4. Turn dough out onto lightly floured counter and sprinkle with a little flour if it feels sticky. The dough should feel soft and have a nice smooth texture. Then transfer the dough into a large glass bowl that has been greased with vegetable oil. Flip the ball of dough over so vegetable oil is on both sides. Then place the glass bowl on the center rack in the slightly warmed oven (make sure the oven is off) for 1 to 2 hours until the dough has risen and doubled in size.

5. Once the dough has doubled in size, punch it 3 to 4 times to release air bubbles, then take it out of the bowl and place on a clean counter. Sprinkle the counter lightly with flour if needed.

6. Line a 9 x 13 baking pan with aluminum foil and grease the bottom and sides with vegetable oil. Make the aluminum foil slightly longer than the baking pan, so you can lift the rolls out of the pan when they are hot.

7. Divide the dough into 16 equal portions and form into balls. Place the dough balls in the baking pan and gently baste with melted butter. Then put them on the center rack in the slightly warmed oven (make sure the oven is off) for about 30 minutes to rise. Once they have risen, remove from the oven. Also remove the pan of water from the bottom rack.

8. Preheat oven to 375 degrees.

9. Place rolls in the oven on the center rack and bake for 20 minutes, or until golden brown. Baste with melted butter and serve.

HOMEMADE HAMBURGER BUNS

INGREDIENTS:

- 3½ Cups All-Purpose Flour (divided)
- ¼ Cup Sugar
- 1 Packet Active Dry Yeast
- 1 Egg (room temperature / beaten)
- ½ Stick Butter (melted and slightly cooled)
- 1 tsp. salt
- 1 Cup Lukewarm Water (divided)
- 1 Tbsp. Vegetable Oil

Egg Wash:

- 1 Egg and 2 Tbsp. Milk (beaten)
- Sesame Seeds (sprinkle on top of each bun)

Prep. time:
90 min

Total time:
30 min

Serves: 4

DIRECTIONS:

1. Pour water into a glass measuring cup and warm in the microwave until the temperature is between 98 to 110 degrees.

2. In a glass bowl, add 1 cup of flour, sugar, egg, butter, yeast, and ½ cup lukewarm water (reserve the remaining ½ cup lukewarm water), and whisk together until blended. Then set aside for 5 to 8 minutes until the yeast activates and bubbles have formed on top of the mixture.

3. In the bowl of a stand mixer, add 2½ cups of flour, and salt. Using the dough hook attachment, mix together on low speed for about 1 minute. Then slowly pour the yeast mixture into the stand mixer bowl and continue to mix until combined with the flour mixture. Slowly add the remaining ½ cup of lukewarm water into the bowl and stop when the dough is sticky and moist looking. Continue to mix on low speed and add little pinches of flour until the dough forms into a ball. Then let it knead for 3 to 5 minutes on low speed.

4. Transfer the dough to a lightly floured work surface and sprinkle with a little flour. The dough should feel soft and smooth. Place the dough in a glass bowl that has been lightly greased with vegetable oil. Cover with a towel and let the dough rise in a warm place for 1 hour.

5. Once the dough has risen, place it on a lightly floured surface and sprinkle with a little flour. Then form into a slightly rounded rectangle shape about ½ inch thick and cut into 8 equal pieces. Then shape each piece into a round hamburger bun and place 1 inch apart on a baking sheet lined with parchment paper. Cover with a towel and let the buns rise for 1 hour.

6. Preheat oven to 350 degrees.

7. Once the buns have risen, gently brush each bun with the egg wash (1 egg and 2 tbsp. milk beaten), and sprinkle with sesame seeds. Then bake at 350 degrees for 20 to 30 minutes, or until golden brown. Let cool on a rack, then slice in half crosswise and serve with your favorite burgers and toppings.

EASY QUICK ROLLS

Prep. time:

5 min

Total time:

12 min

Serves: 4-5

INGREDIENTS:

- 2 Cups Self-Rising Flour
- 1 Cup Milk
- 4 Tbsp. Mayonnaise
- 2 Tsp. Sugar
- ½ - 1 Cup Shredded Cheddar Cheese (optional)

DIRECTIONS:

1. Preheat oven to 450 degrees.

2. In a bowl, add the flour, milk, mayonnaise, and sugar and mix together well. Fold in shredded cheddar cheese (optional).

3. Spray a muffin tin with nonstick baking spray. Spoon the batter into each muffin cup and fill about ¾ full.

4. Bake in the oven for 10 to 12 minutes, or until golden brown. Serve and enjoy these easy delicious rolls with any meal.

SOUTHWEST SKILLET CORNBREAD

INGREDIENTS:

Dry Ingredients:
- 1 Cup All-Purpose Flour
- 1 Cup Yellow Cornmeal
- 1 Tsp. Salt
- 1 Tsp. Baking Powder
- ½ Tsp. Baking Soda
- 2 Tbsp. Sugar

Wet Ingredients:
- 2 Cups Shredded Cheddar Cheese
- 2 Eggs (lightly beaten)
- ¾ Cup Whole Buttermilk
- ⅓ Cup Vegetable Oil
- 1 Cup Cream Style Sweet Corn
- 1 4oz. Can Diced Green Chiles (mild)

Prep. time:
10 min

Total time:
50 min

Serves: 8

DIRECTIONS:

1. Preheat oven to 375 degrees.
2. In a bowl, whisk together the flour, cornmeal, salt, baking powder, baking soda, and sugar.
3. In a separate bowl, mix together the cheese, eggs, buttermilk, vegetable oil, cream style corn, and green chiles.
4. Slowly stir the dry ingredients into the wet ingredients and mix together just until combined.
5. Pour into a 10 inch cast iron skillet sprayed with nonstick cooking spray.
6. Bake in the oven for 50 minutes, or until golden brown and a toothpick inserted in the middle comes out clean.
7. Remove from the oven, cool slightly and serve.

"It is absolutely delicious….so moist, and just the right amount of sweet and spicy!" Steve Hall

SUPER MOIST BANANA BREAD

INGREDIENTS:

- 3 Ripe Bananas
- ½ Tsp. Lemon Juice
- ½ Tsp. Vanilla
- 1 Tbsp. Sour Cream
- 2 Eggs (beaten)
- 1 Stick Butter (softened)
- ½ Cup White Granulated Sugar
- ½ Cup Brown Sugar
- 1½ Cups All-Purpose Flour
- ½ Tsp. Salt
- 1 Tsp. Baking Soda
- 1 Tsp. Cinnamon
- ½ Cup Chopped Black Walnuts

Prep. time:
10 min

Total time:
70 min

Serves: 6

DIRECTIONS:

1. Preheat oven to 325 degrees.

2. In a large bowl, use a fork and mash the ripe bananas until smooth. Then stir in the lemon juice, vanilla, eggs, and sour cream.

3. In another bowl, mix together the softened butter, white sugar, and brown sugar and add to the banana mixture.

4. In a separate bowl, whisk together the flour, salt, baking soda, and cinnamon and slowly stir into the banana mixture until combined. Then fold in the chopped walnuts.

5. Pour into a loaf pan sprayed with nonstick baking spray. Bake for 1 hour and 10 minutes, or until a toothpick inserted in the center comes out clean. Remove from the oven and let cool in the loaf pan for about 10 minutes, then place the banana bread on a wire rack to cool completely.

STEVE'S HUSH PUPPY RECIPE

INGREDIENTS:

- 1 Cup Self-Rising Flour
- 3 Cups Self-Rising Cornmeal Mix
- ½ Cup Sugar
- 1 Tsp. Pepper
- 1 Cup Green Bell Peppers (diced)
- 1 Cup Sweet Onions (finely diced)
- ¾ Cup Frozen Sweet Corn (thawed)
- 1 Tbsp. Diced Jalapeno Peppers
- 2 Eggs (lightly beaten)
- 1 Cup Buttermilk
- 1 Tbsp. Vegetable Oil
- Vegetable Oil for frying

Prep. time:
10 min

Total time:
10 min

Serves: 8

DIRECTIONS:

1. In a bowl, whisk together the self-rising flour, self-rising cornmeal mix, sugar, and pepper. Stir in the green bell peppers, sweet onions, sweet corn, jalapeño peppers, eggs, and vegetable oil. Then slowly stir in the buttermilk and mix until combined and the dough is moist.

2. In a deep frying pan, add 2 - 3 inches of vegetable oil and heat to 360 degrees. Drop the dough by rounded tablespoons in the hot oil and fry in small batches for 2 - 3 minutes, or until golden brown. Then place on a plate lined with paper towels.

3. Serve with your favorite southern meal and enjoy these delicious Hush Puppies...they are crispy on the outside, soft and tender on the inside.

BURGERS AND SANDWICHES

SAN ANTONIO TEX-MEX BURGERS

INGREDIENTS:

- 1 Lb. Ground Beef (80/20)
- 1 Tsp. Salt
- 1 Tsp. Pepper
- 1 Tsp. Garlic Powder
- 1 Tsp. Onion Powder
- 2 Slices Cheddar Cheese
- 2 Tostada Shells or Corn Tortillas
- ½ Cup Refried Beans
- ½ Cup Shredded Cheddar Cheese
- 2 Large Hamburger Buns
- 4 Tbsp. Butter (softened)
- Pico de Gallo

Prep. time:
10 min

Total time:
20 min

Serves:
2

DIRECTIONS:

1. Divide the ground beef into 2 portions (½ lb. each) and shape into hamburger patties. Then place the patties in between 2 sheets of parchment paper and press down until they are about 1 inch thick. In a small bowl, mix together the salt, pepper, garlic powder, and onion powder and sprinkle on both sides of each patty.

2. In a cast iron skillet or griddle on medium heat, cook the patties until they are nicely seared and dark, golden brown on both sides. Then place a slice of cheese on top of each patty and cover to melt the cheese. Transfer the patties to a plate and set aside.

3. Split open each hamburger bun and spread butter on the inside. Then place each half face down in the same cast iron skillet or griddle on medium heat and toast until golden brown. Then place them on a plate and set aside.

4. Preheat oven broiler. Lay the tostada shells (or corn tortillas for a softer tostada) on a nonstick baking sheet. Spread with refried beans and sprinkle with shredded cheddar cheese. Then broil for 3 to 4 minutes, or until the cheese is melted.

5. Put the tostada on the bottom half of each bun and spoon some of the pico de gallo on top. Then top each with a cheddar cheese burger, and then the top of the hamburger bun.

Serve these incredibly delicious burgers with tortilla chips and pico de gallo and enjoy.

BLACK AND BLUE BURGERS

INGREDIENTS:

- Eye of Round Beef Roast
- 1 lb. Ground Beef (80/20)
- 1 Cup Crumbled Blue Cheese
- 1 Sweet Onion (sliced into thin rings)
- 1 Tomato (sliced thin)
- 6 Tbsp. Butter (melted and divided)
- 2 Large Hamburger Buns
- Salt and Black Pepper

Prep. time:
10 min

Total time:
20 min

Serves:
2

DIRECTIONS:

1. Divide 1 lb. of ground beef into 4 portions (¼ lb. each) and shape into hamburger patties. Place the patties in between 2 sheets of parchment paper and press down into thin patties (make each patty a little bigger than the hamburger buns you will be serving them on).

2. Sprinkle 2 patties with black pepper and put crumbled blue cheese on top of each one. Then place a second patty on top of each one and gently press down and seal the edges.

3. Season both sides of the patties with salt and pepper, then place on a grill mat and grill until both sides are deep golden brown. Remove patties and place them on a plate.

4. While the patties are cooking, put the onion rings on the grill mat with 2 tbsp. of butter and cook until they are soft and golden in color. Then place them on the plate with the patties and cover with foil to keep warm.

5. Lightly brush the inside of each hamburger bun with melted butter and toast on the grill mat until golden brown.

6. Place the buns on a plate and put a hamburger patty on each bottom bun, then some grilled onions, and slices of tomato. Cover with the top bun, and you're ready to serve the most flavorful, delicious, juicy hamburgers.

ULTIMATE OPEN-FACED POT ROAST SANDWICH STACKER

Prep. time:
15 min

Total time:
8.5 hours

Serves:
4

INGREDIENTS:

- 1 Beef Chuck Roast (3 - 4 lbs.)
- 1 Packet Beefy Onion Soup Mix
- 1 Packet Savory Pot Roast Seasoning Mix
- 1 Cup Beef Broth
- 1-2 Tbsp. Worcestershire Sauce
- 1 Packet Brown Gravy Mix

Sandwich:

- 4 Slices Texas Toast
- 1 Stick Butter (softened and divided)
- 1 Tbsp. Olive Oil
- 1 Small Can Sliced Mushrooms (drained)
- ½ Cup Sweet Onions (diced)
- 4 Slices Cheddar Cheese (or your choice)
- 1 Package Instant Mashed Potatoes

DIRECTIONS:

1. Place the chuck roast in a crockpot/slow cooker. Sprinkle the beefy onion soup mix and savory pot roast seasoning mix on the chuck roast. Then pour the beef broth and Worcestershire sauce into the crockpot. Cover and cook on high for 6 to 7 hours, or on low for 8 hours.

2. To thicken the gravy, add the beef gravy mix into the crockpot about 20 minutes before the roast has finished cooking. When the chuck roast is done, transfer to a plate and shred it using two forks. Cover and set aside.

3. Prepare instant mashed potatoes according to package directions, then cover and set aside.

4. Spread softened butter on one side of each slice of Texas toast. Then place buttered side down in a skillet and toast on medium heat until golden brown, flip over and toast the other side. Place the slices of toast with the buttered side up on a serving plate and set aside.

5. In a pan on medium heat, add olive oil and 1 tbsp. butter. Once the butter has melted, add the mushrooms and onions and sauté until tender.

6. On each slice of Texas toast, place a slice of cheese, then a scoop of mashed potatoes, then some shredded roast, and drizzle with some brown gravy. Top with some sautéed mushrooms and onions and enjoy!

FRIED TUNA BURGERS

Prep. time: 10 min | Total time: 15 min | Serves: 4

INGREDIENTS:

- 2 5oz. Cans Tuna in Water (drained)
- 1 Egg (lightly beaten)
- 1 Celery Stalk (finely diced)
- ¼ Cup Yellow Onion (finely diced)
- ¾ Cup Breadcrumbs
- ½ Cup Mayonnaise (plus 2 Tbsp. - divided)
- 2 Tbsp. Vegetable Oil
- 4 Tbsp. Softened Butter
- 4 Large Hamburger Buns
- Shredded Iceberg Lettuce
- 1 Tomato Sliced Thin (optional)
- Shredded Cheese (optional)

DIRECTIONS:

1. In a bowl, add the tuna, egg, celery, onion, breadcrumbs, and ½ cup of mayonnaise, and mix together well.

2. Shape evenly into patties the same size as the hamburger buns.

3. In a frying pan on medium heat, add vegetable oil. Then place the tuna patties in the hot pan and fry them until golden brown on both sides. Remove the patties and place them on a plate.

4. Split open the hamburger buns and spread butter on the cut sides of both halves. Then place them buttered side down on the frying pan and toast until golden brown.

5. Set the hamburger buns on a serving plate and put a tuna patty on each bottom bun, then top with shredded lettuce (you can also top with some shredded cheese and sliced tomato), then spread the top hamburger buns with some mayonnaise and place them on top....it's that easy and so good!

FANTASTIC BEER AND WINE BRATS

INGREDIENTS:

- 1 Package Bratwurst Sausages (5 brats)
- 2 Yellow Onions (sliced thin)
- 1 Green Bell Pepper (sliced thin)
- 1 Red Bell Pepper (sliced thin)
- ½ Cup Dijon Mustard
- ¼ Cup Minced Garlic
- 1 Cup Chicken Stock
- 2 Tbsp. Butter
- 1 12oz. Bottle Beer
- ½ Cup Red Wine
- 5 Brat Buns

Toppings:
- Ketchup
- Mustard
- Sauerkraut
- Pickle Relish
- Shredded Cheese

Prep. time:
10 min

Total time:
30 min

Serves: 2-3

DIRECTIONS:

1. In a 5qt. Dutch oven, add onions, green and red bell peppers, Dijon mustard, garlic, butter, and chicken stock. Place on a preheated grill (350 to 400 degrees) and bring to a simmer. Then poke holes on both sides of each brat with a toothpick and place in the Dutch oven. Cover and let simmer for about 5 minutes. Pour in the beer and wine and continue to simmer for 15 minutes.

2. Remove brats from the Dutch oven with tongs and place on the grill. Cook each side 3 to 5 minutes, or until dark golden brown. Then place them back in the Dutch oven and let simmer for about 5 minutes.

3. To serve, place each brat into a bun and top with the cooked onions and peppers, and your choice of ketchup, mustard, sauerkraut, pickle relish, and shredded cheese.

OPEN FACED FISH MELT

Prep. time: 10 min

Total time: 30 min

Serves: 4

INGREDIENTS:

- 4 Cups Flaked White Fish (Crappie, Bluegill or Tilapia Fillets)
- 2 Tbsp. Olive Oil
- 1 Cup Mayonnaise
- ¼ Cup Celery (finely diced)
- 1 Tsp. Red Wine Vinegar
- ½ Tsp. Lemon Juice
- ½ Cup Red or Sweet Onions (finely diced)
- 1 Tsp. Parsley
- 1 Tsp. Sugar
- Salt & Pepper to taste
- 4 Slices Rye Bread (or your choice)
- ½ Slick Butter (softened)
- 1 Large Tomato (sliced)
- 8 Slices Swiss Cheese

DIRECTIONS:

1. Preheat oven to 375 degrees.
2. Drizzle a little olive oil on both sides of each white fish fillet. Then place them on a baking sheet and bake uncovered for about 25 minutes, or until they flake easily with a fork. Remove from the oven and place the fish fillets in a bowl. Then use a fork to flake each fillet apart.
3. Add mayonnaise, celery, red wine vinegar, lemon juice, onions, parsley, and sugar to the flaked fish fillets and mix together until combined. Then season with salt and pepper to taste.
4. Spread softened butter on both sides of the sliced bread, and toast them on a griddle until golden brown. Then place them on a foil lined baking sheet.
5. Spoon the fish mixture evenly on each slice of the toasted bread, then top each with 2 slices of tomatoes, and cover with 2 slices of cheese.
6. Place in the oven and broil for 2 to 3 minutes, or until the cheese is melted and light golden brown. Serve warm and enjoy.

SLOPPY JOES

INGREDIENTS:

- 1½ Lbs. Lean Ground Beef (85/15)
- 1 Medium Yellow Onion (diced)
- 1 Red Bell Pepper (diced)
- 2 Tbsp. Worcestershire Sauce
- 2 Tbsp. Minced Garlic
- 1 Tbsp. Paprika
- 1 Tbsp. Onion Powder
- 1 15oz. Can Tomato Sauce
- 1½ Tsp. Mustard
- 2 Tbsp. Ketchup
- 2 Tbsp. Brown Sugar
- 1 Tsp. Salt
- 1 Stick Butter (softened)
- 4 Sliced Artisan Buns (or your choice)
- 1 Cup Shredded Sharp Cheddar Cheese

DIRECTIONS:

1. In a nonstick skillet on medium heat, add the lean ground beef, onions, and red bell peppers, and cook until ground beef is browned. Then add Worcestershire sauce, minced garlic, paprika, and onion powder. Stir in tomato sauce, mustard, ketchup, brown sugar, and salt. Reduce heat to medium-low and let simmer for about 10 minutes.

2. While the meat mixture is simmering, spread softened butter on the cut side of each bun. In a griddle on medium heat, toast the buns buttered side down until golden brown.

3. Place the toasted buns on a serving plate. Spoon some of the delicious sloppy joe meat mixture on the bottom buns, sprinkle with shredded cheddar cheese, and then the tops of the buns and serve.

Prep. time: 10 min | Total time: 20 min | Serves: 4

CRISPY BEER BATTERED FISH SANDWICH

INGREDIENTS:

- 6 Cod Fillets (or your choice of white fish)
- 2 Cups All-Purpose Flour (divided)
- ¼ Cup Cornstarch
- 4 Tsp. Seafood Seasoning
- ½ Tsp. Baking Powder
- 1 Cup Cold Beer
- Vegetable Oil (for frying)
- Artesano/Brioche Bakery Buns
- Mayonnaise
- Bread & Butter Pickles (thin sliced stackers)
- Coleslaw

Tartar Sauce:

- 1½ Cups Mayonnaise
- 1 Cup Sweet Pickle Relish (drained)
- ½ Cup finely diced Sweet Onions
- 1 Tsp. Mustard
- ½ Tsp. Lemon Juice
- ½ Tsp. Apple Cider Vinegar
- 1 Dash of Cajun Seasoning
- Mix all ingredients together and chill until ready to serve.

Prep. time:
10 min

Total time:
10 min

Serves: 4-6

DIRECTIONS:

1. In a shallow bowl, add 1 cup all-purpose flour. Then dredge each fish fillet in the flour, place on a plate and let set for about 10 minutes.

2. Make a beer batter: In a bowl, add 1 cup all-purpose flour, cornstarch, seafood seasoning, and baking powder, and mix together. Slowly add very cold beer and stir until the batter is like the consistency of pancake batter.

3. In a deep fry pan on medium heat, add vegetable oil (about 1½ inch deep) and heat it to 350 degrees. Dip each flour coated fish fillet, one at a time, into the beer batter. Then place in the frying pan and cook for about 2 to 3 minutes per side, or until golden brown on both sides (only fry a few fillets at a time so the pan is not overcrowded). Then place them on a plate lined with paper towels.

4. Split open each bun and lightly spread mayonnaise on the inside of both halves. Then place each half face down on a griddle on medium heat and toast until light golden brown.

5. Spread tartar sauce on each of the bottom buns, then put a couple of thin sliced sandwich pickles, then a fried fish fillet, a heaping spoonful of coleslaw, and then the top of the bun. Serve and enjoy!

CASSEROLES

7 CHEESE BAKED MAC AND CHEESE

Prep. time: 10 min | Total time: 40 min | Serves: 6

INGREDIENTS:

- 1 16oz. Box Large Elbow Macaroni
- 6 Cups Vegetable Broth
- 6 Cups Water
- 2 Tsp. Salt
- ½ Stick Butter (melted)
- ¼ Cup Heavy Whipping Cream
- 1 Tsp. Sugar
- 2 Eggs (beaten)
- ¼ Cup Cream Cheese
- ½ Cup Mozzarella Cheese (shredded)
- ½ Cup Sharp Cheddar Cheese (shredded)
- ½ Cup Parmesan Cheese (shredded)
- ½ Cup Monterey Jack Cheese (shredded)
- 1 8oz. Tub Small Curd Cottage Cheese
- 1 Tsp. Worcestershire Sauce
- 1 Tsp. Hot Sauce
- 8 Slices Colby-Jack Cheese

DIRECTIONS:

1. Preheat oven to 350 degrees.
2. In a large pot or Dutch oven on medium heat, bring 6 cups of vegetable broth and 6 cups of water to a boil. Then add salt, and stir in the elbow macaroni. Boil uncovered for about 5 to 7 minutes (stirring every couple of minutes) until the macaroni is al dente, then drain.
3. Pour the macaroni while it is still hot into a large bowl and stir in the melted butter, heavy whipping cream, sugar, and eggs. Then stir in the cream cheese, mozzarella cheese, cheddar cheese, parmesan cheese, Monterey jack cheese, cottage cheese, Worcestershire sauce, and hot sauce.
4. Spoon the macaroni and cheese mixture into a casserole dish sprayed with nonstick cooking spray. Then top with slices of Colby-Jack cheese.
5. Bake uncovered in the oven for 20 to 25 minutes, or until the cheese has melted and is golden brown.

"Wait till you taste all these flavors together. It's absolutely fantastic" Steve Hall

DELICIOUS FISH CASSEROLE

INGREDIENTS:

- 2 Cups Baked and Flaked White Fish (Crappie or Tilapia Fillets, or your choice)
- 1 16oz. Bag Extra Wide Egg Noodles
- 2 Tsp. Salt
- ½ Cup Diced Sweet Onions
- 1 Cup Frozen Peas (thawed)
- 1½ Cups Mushrooms (quartered)
- 3 Tbsp. Olive Oil (divided)
- 2 Tbsp. Butter
- 3 Cups Shredded Mexican Style Blend Cheese
- 2 Cans Condensed Cream of Mushroom Soup
- ¼ Cup Half and Half
- Salt and Pepper to taste

Topping:

- 2 Cups Crushed Butter Crackers
- 1 Stick Butter (melted)

Prep. time:	Total time:	Serves:
10 min	90 min	4-6

Steve Hall

DIRECTIONS:

1. Preheat oven to 350 degrees.

2. Baste both sides of each white fish fillet lightly with some olive oil and season with salt and pepper. Then bake them in the oven on a baking sheet uncovered at 350 degrees for about 25 minutes, or until they flake apart with a fork. Remove from the oven and place the fish fillets in a bowl. Flake each fillet apart using a fork, then set aside.

3. Bring a large pot filled ¾ full of water to a boil on medium heat. Add egg noodles and 2 tsp. of salt and boil (stirring occasionally) until almost done, or al dente (about 2 to 3 minutes less than package suggested cooking time). Then drain and set aside.

4. In a skillet on medium heat, add 1 tbsp. olive oil and 2 tbsp. butter. Once butter has melted, add mushrooms and sauté until tender. Season with salt and pepper, then remove from heat and set aside.

5. In a large bowl, add the flaked fish fillets, onions, peas, mushrooms, and 1 cup of the shredded cheese. Stir in the cream of mushroom soup and half and half. Then fold the egg noodles in a little at a time until coated with the mixture.

6. Pour mixture into a 9 x 13 casserole dish sprayed with nonstick cooking spray and sprinkle with the remaining 2 cups of shredded cheese. In a small bowl, mix together the crushed butter crackers and 1 stick of melted butter and spread evenly on top of the casserole.

7. Cover with aluminum foil and bake in the oven at 350 degrees for 30 minutes, then remove the foil and continue baking for 20 to 30 minutes, or until bubbly and the butter cracker topping is golden brown.

ONE PAN BEEFY ONION RING CASSEROLE

Prep. time: 10 min | Total time: 60 min | Serves: 4

INGREDIENTS:

- 1½ lbs. Ground Beef (85/15)
- 1 Medium Yellow Onion (chopped)
- ½ Cup Mushrooms (sliced into quarters)
- 1½ Tsp. Garlic Salt
- 2 Tbsp. Ketchup
- 2 Tbsp. Worcestershire Sauce
- 1 Can Condensed Cream of Mushroom Soup
- 1 12oz. Bag Frozen Mixed Vegetables (thawed)
- 1 16oz. Bag Frozen Potatoes O'Brien (thawed)
- 1 Bag Frozen Breaded Onion Rings
- ½ Stick Butter (melted)
- 1 Cup Sharp Cheddar Cheese (shredded)

DIRECTIONS:

1. Preheat oven to 350 degrees.

2. In a cast iron skillet on medium heat, add the ground beef and the onions. Break the ground beef up into smaller pieces with a spatula or spoon and cook until the beef is browned and onions are soft. Season the ground beef with garlic salt.

3. Then add the ketchup, Worcestershire sauce, mushrooms, condensed cream of mushroom soup, and mixed vegetables into the skillet with the ground beef and mix together well.

4. Spread the beef mixture evenly in the skillet Then add a layer of the Potatoes O'Brien and drizzle the melted butter evenly across the top. Sprinkle with the shredded cheddar cheese and top with a layer of the breaded onion rings.

5. Place in the oven and bake for 30 to 40 minutes, or until the onion rings are brown and crispy and the cheese has melted. Serve and enjoy this easy, delicious one pan casserole.

CHEESY CHICKEN NOODLE SOUP CASSEROLE

Prep. time:
10 min

Total time:
30 min

Serves:
6

INGREDIENTS:

- 1 12oz. Pkg. Wide Egg Noodles
- 1 Stick Butter
- 1 Yellow Onion (diced)
- ½ Cup Celery (diced)
- 3 Tbsp. Minced Garlic
- ¼ Cup All-Purpose Flour
- 2 Cups Chicken Broth
- 2 Cups Whole Milk
- ¼ Tsp. Salt
- ¼ Tsp. Black Pepper
- 2 Cups Frozen Mixed Vegetables (thawed)
- 2 Cups Cooked and Shredded Chicken
- 2 Cups Sharp Cheddar Cheese (shredded)

Toppings:

- 1 Cup Sharp Cheddar Cheese (shredded)
- 1 Cup Butter Crackers (crushed - we use Ritz)
- ¼ Cup Grated Parmesan Cheese
- 4 Tbsp. Butter (melted)

DIRECTIONS:

1. Preheat oven to 400 degrees.
2. Fill a large pot with water and bring to a boil. Add the egg noodles and cook until al dente (about 2 minutes less than package directions). Drain and pour the noodles into a 9 x 13 casserole dish sprayed with nonstick cooking spray.
3. In a large skillet on medium heat, add 1 stick of butter. Once the butter has melted, add the onions, and celery, and sauté until tender. Stir in minced garlic and flour and cook for 1 minute. Then slowly pour in the chicken broth and milk, season with salt and pepper, and bring to a simmer, stirring constantly until thickened.
4. Once the mixture has thickened, stir in the mixed vegetables, shredded chicken, and cheddar cheese. Remove from heat and stir until the cheese has melted. Pour the mixture over the egg noodles in the casserole dish.
5. Top with the shredded cheddar cheese, then the crushed butter crackers, and grated parmesan cheese, and drizzle with melted butter.
6. Place in the oven and bake uncovered for 15 minutes, or until the cheese and butter cracker topping is golden brown.

SEVEN LAYER CHICKEN ENCHILADA CASSEROLE

INGREDIENTS:

- 1 Rotisserie Chicken (3 cups shredded)
- 1 Packet Taco Seasoning Mix
- 8 Large Flour Tortillas
- 4 Cups Shredded Mexican Style Blend Cheese
- 1 16oz. Can Refried Beans
- 1 15oz. Jar Medium Queso Blanco Cheese Dip
- 1 8.8oz. Pouch 90 Second Spanish Style Ready Rice
- 1 10oz. Can Diced Tomatoes with Lime and Cilantro
- 1½ Cups Pico de Gallo
- 1 19oz. Can Mild Red Enchilada Sauce
- 1 2.2oz. Can Sliced Black Olives (drained)
- ½ Cup Chopped Green Onions
- 1 Tbsp. Olive Oil
- Nonstick Cooking Spray

Prep. time:
15 min

Total time:
40 min

Serves: 6

DIRECTIONS:

1. Preheat oven to 350 degrees.
2. In a large skillet on medium heat, add olive oil. Once the olive oil is hot, place the shredded chicken in the skillet and season with the packet of taco seasoning. Stir in 4 tbsp. of the enchilada sauce, and a little scoop of Pico de Gallo. Let simmer for about 3 to 4 minutes, then remove from heat.
3. In a 9 x 13 casserole dish sprayed with nonstick cooking spray, spread a few spoonfuls of enchilada sauce in the bottom, then place 4 tortillas in the bottom of the casserole dish (they can overlap so they cover the entire bottom and up the sides of the dish).
4. Pour the chicken mixture on the tortillas and spread it evenly in the casserole dish with a spoon. Then add a layer of refried beans, diced tomatoes with lime and cilantro, Spanish style rice, queso blanco cheese dip, Pico de Gallo, and 2 cups of the shredded cheese. Add a final layer of tortillas on top, then pour the remaining can of enchilada sauce evenly over the tortillas. Top with the remaining 2 cups of shredded cheese, and then the black olives and green onions.
5. Bake uncovered for 35 to 40 minutes, or until the cheese has melted and lightly golden brown. Then remove from the oven and let it sit for about 10 minutes before serving.

CHILI, SOUPS AND STEWS

CREAMY CHICKEN POTATO SOUP

INGREDIENTS:

- 6 - 8 Skinless Boneless Chicken Thighs (cut into cubes)
- 4 Tbsp. Olive Oil (divided)
- 7 Tbsp. Butter (divided)
- 5 Tbsp. All-Purpose Flour
- 6 Carrots (peeled and sliced)
- 3 Celery Stalks (finely diced)
- 5 Gold Potatoes (cut into small chunks)
- 1 Medium Yellow Onion (diced)
- 1 Tbsp. Minced Garlic
- 4 Cups Chicken Broth
- 1½ Cups Half and Half
- 2 Cups Whole Milk
- 1 Tbsp. Granulated Chicken Bouillon
- ½ Tsp. Paprika
- ½ Tsp. Onion Powder
- ¼ Tsp. Red Pepper Flakes
- ½ Tsp. Black Pepper
- 2 Tbsp. Fresh Parsley (chopped)
- 2 Dried Bay Leaves
- Salt and Pepper to taste
- Garnish with Shredded Cheese and Fresh Chopped Parsley

Prep. time: 15 min

Total time: 60 min

Serves: 6

DIRECTIONS:

1. Cut the chicken up into evenly sized cubes or bite size pieces. In a Dutch oven on medium heat, add 2 tbsp. olive oil. Place chicken in the pot and season with salt and pepper. Cook for about 8 to 10 minutes (stirring frequently). Then remove the chicken and set aside on a plate (chicken will finish cooking when added into the soup).

2. In the same pot, add 2 tbsp. olive oil and 2 tbsp. butter. Once the butter has melted, add the onions, carrots, and celery and sauté about 8 to 10 minutes, or until the vegetables are tender. Then stir in the minced garlic and sauté for 1 more minute.

3. Melt 5 tbsp. butter in the pot with the vegetables, then stir in 5 tbsp. flour and cook for about 2 minutes (stirring continuously). Slowly pour in the chicken broth, half and half, and milk, and stir to combine.

4. Add the chicken back into the pot. Then add the potatoes, chicken bouillon, paprika, onion powder, red pepper flakes, black pepper, parsley, and the bay leaves. Turn the heat down to low, cover and simmer for about 30 to 35 minutes (stirring occasionally), or until the potatoes are fork tender. Season with salt and pepper to taste and remove the bay leaves. Serve and garnish with shredded cheese and fresh parsley.

WESTERN BACON CHEESEBURGER SOUP

Prep. time: 15 min

Total time: 75 min

Serves: 4

INGREDIENTS:

- 1 lb. Bacon (chopped / divided)
- 2 lbs. Ground Beef (80/20)
- 1 Medium Yellow Onion (diced)
- 1 Tbsp. Minced Garlic
- 1 Tsp. Salt
- 1 Tsp. Pepper
- ½ Tsp. Onion Powder
- ½ Tsp. Garlic Powder
- 1 Tbsp. Worcestershire Sauce
- 2 Tbsp. Barbecue Sauce
- 1 Tsp. Mustard
- ½ Cup All-Purpose Flour
- 1 Cup Mushrooms (sliced)
- 1 Can Diced Tomatoes (drained)
- 4 Cups Beef Broth
- 2 Cups Whole Milk
- ½ Block Cream Cheese
- 3 Cups Shredded Sharp Cheddar Cheese

Toppings:
- Shredded Cheese (white and yellow cheddar cheese)
- Dill Pickles (chopped)
- Crumbled Bacon

DIRECTIONS:

1. In a Dutch oven on medium heat, add chopped bacon and cook until crispy. Remove bacon with a slotted spoon and place in a bowl. Then set aside.

2. Add the ground beef and onions into the Dutch oven with the bacon drippings and cook on medium heat until the beef is browned, and onions are tender. Then add the minced garlic, salt, pepper, garlic powder, onion powder, Worcestershire sauce, barbecue sauce, and mustard.

3. Stir all-purpose flour into the meat mixture and cook for about 1 minute. Add the mushrooms and diced tomatoes, and continue to cook for another 3 to 5 minutes. Then add the chopped bacon (reserve about ½ cup for topping).

4. Add in the beef broth, milk, cream cheese, and shredded sharp cheddar cheese and stir to combine. Then cover and simmer on medium-low heat for 20 to 30 minutes (stirring occasionally). Season with salt and pepper to taste.

5. Serve in a bowl and top with shredded cheese, chopped dill pickles, crumbled bacon, and crispy fried onions. So delicious, creamy, and cheesy!

BEER HOT DOG CHILI

Prep. time:
15 min

Total time:
45 min

Serves: 5

INGREDIENTS:

- 1 lb. Ground Beef (80/20)
- ½ Cup Sweet Onions (diced)
- 1 Tsp. Red Pepper Flakes
- 1 Tsp. Black Pepper
- ½ Tsp. Salt
- ½ Tsp. Oregano
- 1 Tbsp. Onion Powder
- 1 Tbsp. Garlic Powder
- ½ Tsp. Ground Cumin
- 1 Tbsp. Chili Powder
- 1 10oz. Can Mild Diced Tomatoes and Chilies
- 3 Tbsp. Tomato Paste
- ½ Tsp. Worcestershire Sauce
- 2 Tbsp. Brown Sugar
- ½ Bottle of Beer (your choice)

DIRECTIONS:

1. In a cast iron skillet on medium heat, add the ground beef and use a spatula or spoon to break it up into small pieces while it is cooking. Then add the onions and cook until the ground beef is browned and the onions are tender.

2. In a small bowl, mix together the red pepper flakes, black pepper, salt, oregano, onion powder, garlic powder, cumin, and chili powder. Then sprinkle the seasoning mixture on the ground beef.

3. Stir in the diced tomatoes and chilies, tomato paste, Worcestershire sauce, brown sugar, and beer. Turn the heat down to low and simmer for 30 to 40 minutes and it's ready to serve.

END OF SUMMER HAMBURGER VEGGIE STEW

Prep. time:
15 min

Total time:
6-7 hours

Serves: 6

INGREDIENTS:

- 2 Lbs. Ground Beef (85/15)
- 1 Cup Sweet Onions (diced / divided)
- 4 Large Tomatoes (chopped)
- 2 Cups Green Beans (cut in 1 inch pieces)
- 2 Zucchinis (chopped)
- 2 Yellow Summer Squash (chopped)
- 2 Cups Beef Broth
- 1 Small Can Tomato Sauce
- 2 Tsp. Salt
- 2 Tsp. Pepper
- 2 Tsp. Garlic Powder
- 2 Tsp Onion Powder
- 2 Tsp. Parsley
- ½ Tsp. Red Pepper Flakes

DIRECTIONS:

1. In a skillet on medium heat, add the ground beef and ½ cup onions. Cook until the ground beef is browned. Then season with (1 tsp. of each) salt, pepper, garlic powder, and onion powder. Remove from heat and set aside.

2. In a crockpot, add the tomatoes, green beans, zucchini, summer squash, and ½ cup onions.

3. Add the cooked ground beef into the crockpot. Then pour in the beef broth and tomato sauce. Season with (1 tsp. of each) salt, pepper, garlic powder, and onion powder. Then sprinkle in the parsley and red pepper flakes. Stir to combine.

4. Cover and cook on high for 4 to 5 hours, or on low for 6 to 7 hours.

5. Serve this delicious comfort food in a bowl garnished with grated parmesan cheese, or shredded cheese of your choice along with some warm buttered biscuits and enjoy.

DILL PICKLE SOUP

Prep. time: 15 min

Total time: 20 min

Serves: 6

INGREDIENTS:

- 2¾ Cups Chicken Broth
- ¼ Cup Unsalted Butter (melted)
- 1 Cup Finely Diced Carrots
- 1 lb. Potatoes (diced into small chunks)
- ½ Cup Finely Diced Dill Pickles
- 1 Cup Dill Pickle Juice
- ½ Cup Sour Cream
- ¼ Cup All-Purpose Flour
- ⅛ Cup Water
- ¼ Tsp. Salt
- ¼ Tsp. Cayenne Pepper
- ½ Tsp. Seafood Seasoning

Garnish:
- Fresh Dill and Thin Sliced Dill Pickles

DIRECTIONS:

1. In a Dutch oven on medium heat, add chicken broth, melted butter, carrots, and potatoes. Bring to a boil, then cover and cook for about 5 to 10 minutes, or until potatoes are fork tender. Add the diced dill pickles and continue to boil for 1 or 2 more minutes.

2. In a small bowl, whisk together the sour cream, flour, and ⅛ cup water to make a paste. Then whisk into the soup a little at a time. Reduce heat to medium-low and simmer (stirring continuously) until the soup is smooth and creamy.

3. Season with salt, cayenne pepper, and seafood seasoning. Then stir in the dill pickle juice and let simmer for about 5 minutes.

4. Serve and garnish with fresh dill and thin slices of dill pickles. You can also sprinkle some shredded cheese on top!

CORN CHOWDER

Prep. time: 15 min | Total time: 45 min | Serves: 6

INGREDIENTS:

- 6 Slices Bacon (cut into small pieces)
- 3 Tbsp. Butter
- 1 Sweet Onion (diced)
- 3 Tbsp. All-Purpose Flour
- 3 Cups Chicken Broth
- 8 Small Yukon Gold Potatoes (cut into quarters or cubes)
- 1 Tsp. Salt
- ½ Tsp. Pepper
- 1½ Cups Whole Milk
- 1½ Cups Heavy Cream
- 3 Cans Whole Kernel Sweet Corn (drained)
- 2 Tsp. Sugar
- 1 Cup Shredded Cheddar Cheese (for garnish)

DIRECTIONS:

1. In a Dutch oven on medium heat, cook bacon until crisp. Remove with a slotted spoon and place on a plate lined with paper towels and set aside. Drain the bacon grease leaving about 1 tbsp. in the pot and add butter. Once the butter has melted, add the onions and sauté about 4 minutes, or until tender.

2. Stir in flour and cook for 1 to 2 minutes. Then whisk in the chicken broth and bring to a boil. Add potatoes, salt, and pepper. Reduce heat to medium low. Partially cover and let simmer for about 15 to 20 minutes, or until the potatoes are fork tender.

3. Add in the milk, heavy cream, corn, and sugar, and gently stir until combined. Cover and let simmer for 5 to 8 minutes, stirring occasionally.

4. Serve hot and garnish with shredded cheddar cheese and crumbled bacon.

SLOW COOKER CHUNKY CHICKEN STEW

INGREDIENTS:

- 3 Chicken Breasts (boneless/skinless - cut into large chunks)
- 1 Bag (1 ½ lb.) Petite Gold Potatoes (sliced in half)
- 1 16oz. Bag Cut & Peeled Baby Carrots (cut in half)
- 1 Cup Sliced Celery
- 1 Cup Mushrooms (sliced in half)
- 1 Sweet Onion (chopped)
- 1 15oz. Can Diced Tomatoes
- 1 8oz. Can Tomato Puree
- 1 Tbsp. Minced Garlic
- 1 Tsp. Granulated Chicken Bouillon
- 2 Bay Leaves
- 1 Tsp. Salt
- 1 Tsp. Pepper
- 1 Tsp. Garlic Powder
- 1 Tsp. Onion Powder
- 1 Tsp. Paprika
- ½ Tsp. Dried Thyme
- 1 32oz. Box Chicken Broth

Slurry:
- ⅔ Cups Cold Water
- 6 Tbsp. Cornstarch

Garnish:
- Shredded Parmesan Cheese and Parsley

Prep. time: 15 min | Total time: 6-8 hours | Serves: 6

DIRECTIONS:

1. In a large crockpot/slow cooker sprayed with nonstick cooking spray, place the potatoes, carrots, celery, mushrooms, and onions in the bottom, then place the chicken on top of the vegetables. Add the diced tomatoes, tomato puree, minced garlic, granulated chicken bouillon, and bay leaves. Season with salt, pepper, garlic powder, onion powder, paprika, and thyme. Then pour in the chicken broth. Cover and cook on high for 4 to 6 hours, or low for 8 hours.

2. Make the slurry about 30 minutes before the stew has finished cooking. In a small bowl, whisk together the water and cornstarch until smooth. Then stir the slurry into the stew, cover and continue to cook for about 30 minutes, or until the stew thickens and vegetables are tender.

3. Garnish with shredded parmesan cheese and parsley and serve with slices of buttered bread.

COWBOY STEW

INGREDIENTS:

- 6 Slices Bacon (cut into 1-inch pieces)
- 1 14oz. Package Smoked Sausage (sliced into ½-inch round pieces)
- 1½ Lbs. Lean Ground Beef (85/15)
- 1 Medium Sweet Onion (diced)
- 3 Tbsp. Garlic (minced)
- 1 Tsp. Salt
- 1 Tsp. Garlic Powder
- 1 Tsp. Onion Powder
- 1 Tsp. Black Pepper
- 1 Tsp. Chili Powder
- 3 Tbsp. All-Purpose Flour
- 2 Cans Diced Tomatoes with Mild Green Chilies
- 2 22oz. Cans Beans (Grillin' Smokehouse Tradition)
- 1 15oz. Can Sweet Corn (drained)
- 3 Russet Potatoes (peeled and cubed)
- 2 Cups Beef Broth
- 2 Tbsp. Parsley (chopped)

Prep. time: 15 min | Total time: 75 min | Serves: 6

DIRECTIONS:

1. In a Dutch oven or large pot on medium heat, add chopped bacon and cook until brown and crispy. Using a slotted spoon, transfer bacon to a plate lined with paper towels.
2. Turn heat down to medium low, then add sausage into the bacon drippings and cook until lightly browned on both sides. Remove from the pot and place on a plate lined with paper towels and set aside.
3. Turn the heat back up to medium and add lean ground beef and onions. Cook until ground beef is browned, then add minced garlic and cook for another minute. Season with salt, pepper, garlic powder, onion powder, and chili powder. Then stir in flour and cook for about 2 minutes.
4. Add diced tomatoes and green chilies, beans, sweet corn, potatoes, bacon, sausage, and beef broth. Bring to a boil, then immediately reduce heat to low. Cover and simmer for 30 to 45 minutes, stirring occasionally.
5. Garnish with parsley and serve with some cornbread. Absolutely delicious!

DINNERTIME FAVORITES

SALISBURY STEAK AND MUSHROOM GRAVY

Prep. time: 15 min | Total time: 45 min | Serves: 6

INGREDIENTS:

- 2 Lbs. Ground Beef (80/20)
- 1 Cup Breadcrumbs
- 1 Egg
- 3 Tbsp. Ketchup
- 2 Tbsp. Worcestershire Sauce
- 2 Tbsp. Dried Onion Flakes
- 1 Tsp. Onion Powder
- 1 Tsp. Garlic Powder
- 1 Tsp. Salt
- 1 Tsp. Pepper

Mushroom Gravy:
- 2 Tbsp. Olive Oil
- 1 Medium Chopped Yellow Onion
- 2 Cups Sliced Mushrooms
- 2 Tbsp. Minced Garlic
- 4 Tbsp. Butter
- 4 Tbsp. Flour
- 4 Cups Beef Broth
- 1 Tbsp. Worcestershire Sauce
- Salt and Pepper to taste

DIRECTIONS:

1. In a bowl, mix together the ground beef, breadcrumbs, egg, ketchup, Worcestershire sauce, onion flakes, onion powder, garlic powder, salt and pepper. Divide into 6 portions and shape into oval patties.

2. In a skillet on medium-high heat, brown both sides of the patties (about 2 minutes on each side) until partially cooked. Remove patties from the pan and set aside on a plate.

3. To make the mushroom gravy: In the same skillet on medium heat, add olive oil to the drippings and sauté the onions and mushrooms. Cook for about 5 minutes, or until onions are translucent, then add minced garlic and cook for another minute. Add butter to the skillet and melt. Then add the flour and cook for 2 to 3 minutes. Slowly stir in the beef broth and add the Worcestershire sauce. Season with salt and pepper and bring the gravy to a simmer.

4. Then add the patties back into the pan with the gravy. Turn the heat down to low, and cover and simmer for 20 minutes, occasionally basting the patties with the gravy. Flip the patties over and baste with the gravy. Cover and continue cooking for about 20 more minutes, or until the patties are cooked through.

5. Serve this delicious homemade Salisbury Steak with Mushroom Gravy over mashed potatoes along with your favorite veggie and enjoy!

ONE PAN PEPPER STEAK

Prep. time: 15 min | Total time: 25 min | Serves: 4

INGREDIENTS:

- 1 Top Sirloin Steak (partially thawed)
- 1 Tsp. Black Pepper
- ½ Cup Beef Broth
- 4 Tbsp. Soy Sauce
- 2 Tbsp. Brown Sugar
- 2 Tbsp. Cornstarch
- ¼ Cup Water
- 1 Small Yellow Onion (chopped)
- 3 Tbsp. Minced Garlic
- 1 Tsp. Ground Ginger
- 1 Green Bell Pepper (sliced thin)
- 1 Red Bell Pepper (sliced thin)
- 1 Small Carrot (sliced thin)
- 3 Tbsp. Sesame or Olive Oil
- White Rice (cooked according to package directions)

DIRECTIONS:

Sauce Directions:

1. In a bowl, whisk together the beef broth, soy sauce, and brown sugar.
2. In a separate small bowl, mix the cornstarch with ¼ cup of water to make a slurry. Pour it into the bowl with the sauce mixture and add black pepper and whisk together until well combined. Then set aside.

Steak and Vegetable Directions:

3. Place the partially thawed sirloin steak on a cutting board and sprinkle generously with black pepper on both sides of the steak. Slice into thin strips against the grain (leaving the steak partially thawed makes it easier to slice into thin strips).
4. In a skillet on medium-high heat add sesame oil. Once the oil is hot, add beef strips and cook until seared on both sides.
5. Add a little more oil if needed in the skillet, then add in the onion, garlic, ground ginger, green and red bell peppers, and carrot slices, and cook until the veggies are tender.
6. Turn the heat down to medium. Then pour in the sauce mixture, bring it to a simmer and cook until the sauce thickens.
7. Serve over a bed of white rice and enjoy...it is so easy to make and delicious!

GRILLED JAMAICAN JERK CHICKEN

INGREDIENTS:
- 8 Chicken Pieces (Thighs and Drumsticks)

Marinade:
- ½ Cup Canola Oil
- ⅓ Cup Apple Cider Vinegar
- ⅓ Cup Soy Sauce
- ½ Cup Orange Juice
- 3 Tbsp. Chopped Garlic
- 2 Tbsp. Fresh Grated Ginger Root
- 1 Cup Red Onions (chopped)
- ⅓ Cup Green Onions (chopped)
- 1 to 3 Scotch Bonnet Peppers (chopped with no seeds (or 1 to 3 Tsp. Scotch Bonnet Pepper Sauce)
- ¼ Cup Lime Juice

Seasoning:
- 1 Tbsp. Paprika
- 3 Tsp. Ground Allspice
- 2 Tsp. Salt
- 1 Tbsp. Black Pepper
- 2 Tbsp. Brown Sugar
- 1½ Tsp. Cinnamon
- 1 Tsp. Ground Coriander
- ½ Tsp. Ground Cloves
- 3 Tsp. Ground Thyme

Basting Sauce:
- ¼ of the Reserved Marinade Sauce
- 2 Tbsp. Honey
- ¼ Cup Brown Sugar
- ¼ Cup Soy Sauce

Prep. time:
24 hours

Total time:
60 min

Serves: 4

DIRECTIONS:

1. Place the chicken thighs and drumsticks on a cutting board. Using a sharp knife, cut 2 small slices on the skin side of each piece.

2. In a blender or food processor, add all the marinade and seasoning ingredients. Then pulse together until well blended. Place the chicken pieces in a 1 gallon resealable food storage bag and pour ¾ of the marinade sauce over the chicken. Seal the bag and place it in the refrigerator for 4 to 24 hours. Pour the remaining ¼ of the marinade sauce into a bowl (it will be used to make the basting sauce), then cover and place in the refrigerator.

3. Remove the bag of marinated chicken from the refrigerator about 30 minutes before grilling them. Also remove the bowl of the reserved marinade sauce and set aside. Then place the marinated chicken pieces on a hot oiled grill and cook until both sides are lightly charred. Cover and continue to grill the chicken, checking and turning often, until the chicken is cooked through and the internal temperature reaches 165 degrees.

4. To make the basting sauce: Add honey, brown sugar, and soy sauce into the bowl of the reserved marinade sauce. Mix together until well blended. Baste the chicken on both sides with the basting sauce and grill for a few more minutes.

CHICKEN FRIED CHICKEN AND HOMEMADE GRAVY

INGREDIENTS:

- 3 - 4 Boneless/Skinless Chicken Breasts (sliced in half horizontally and pounded)
- Vegetable Oil (for frying)

Dry Mixture:
- 2½ Cups All-Purpose Flour
- 1 Tsp. Salt
- 1 Tsp. Pepper
- 1 Tsp. Paprika
- 1 Tsp. Garlic Powder

Wet Mixture:
- 2 Eggs
- 1 Cup Whole Buttermilk

Gravy:
- 8 Tbsp. Oil/Pan Drippings
- ½ Cup All-Purpose Flour
- ½ Tsp. Salt
- ½ Tsp. Pepper
- 1 12oz. Can Evaporated Milk
- 2 Tsp. Granulated Chicken Bouillon (dissolve in ¼ cup of hot water)
- 1 16oz Bottle of Water

Prep. time: 15 min

Total time: 55 min

Serves: 6

DIRECTIONS:

1. Place chicken breast on a cutting board and slice each piece in half horizontally. Then place the chicken pieces between 2 sheets of parchment paper. Use the flat side of a meat mallet and gently pound until the pieces are even in thickness (about ¼ to ½ inch thick).

2. For the chicken you will need 2 shallow bowls for the wet and dry mixture you will be coating them with. In bowl #1, whisk together the 1½ cups flour, and 1 tsp. each of salt, pepper, paprika, and garlic powder. In bowl #2, whisk together the eggs and buttermilk.

3. Dip the chicken pieces in the egg/buttermilk mixture, then dredge in the flour mixture. Repeat this step one more time, then lay the pieces on a rack and let them rest for about 10 minutes.

4. In a frying pan on medium heat, pour in vegetable oil (about ¼ inch deep) and bring to 350 degrees.

5. Fry the chicken until golden brown on both sides, then place them on a rack while making the gravy.

6. To make the gravy: In a small bowl whisk together ½ cup flour, and ½ tsp. each of salt and pepper. In a separate small bowl, mix the 2 tsp. of granulated chicken bouillon and ¼ cup of hot water. Keep about 8 tablespoons of the oil/pan drippings in the frying pan and turn the heat to medium. Then whisk the flour mixture into the oil/pan drippings and cook the flour for about 2 – 3 minutes, whisking constantly. Then slowly add the evaporated milk, granulated chicken bouillon, and water, and continue to whisk and simmer for about 3 minutes. Once the gravy thickens, season with salt and pepper to taste.

7. Serve the chicken smothered with heaping spoonfuls of the delicious creamy gravy along with mashed potatoes and your favorite veggie and enjoy!

ROASTED CHICKEN, SAUSAGE, PEPPERS AND POTATOES

INGREDIENTS:

- 5 Italian Sausage Links (Hot, Mild or Sweet)
- 8 Chicken Thighs
- 7 Tbsp. Olive Oil (divided)
- 6 Mini Sweet Peppers (mixed colors - sliced and seeded)
- 2 Bell Peppers (1 Green and 1 Red – sliced and seeded)
- 1 Red Onion (sliced)
- 1 Yellow Onion (sliced)
- 1½ Lbs. Petite Yukon Gold Potatoes
- 1 Tsp. Salt
- 1 Tsp. Ground Black Pepper
- 1 Tsp. Garlic Powder
- 1 Tsp. Onion Powder
- 2 Tsp. Basil
- 1 Tsp. Paprika
- 1 Tsp. Italian Seasoning
- ½ Tsp. Red Pepper Flakes
- 1 Tsp. Fresh Thyme
- Garnish with Fresh Parsley (chopped)

Prep. time: 20 min | Total time: 75 min | Serves: 4

Jennifer Bruce & Miss Sheila

DIRECTIONS:

1. Preheat oven to 450 degrees.

2. In a nonstick frying pan on medium heat, add 2 tbsp. olive oil. Place the Italian sausage links in the pan and cook just until browned, then flip them over and brown the other side (only cook about 3 minutes per side to brown, they will finish cooking in the oven). Pierce one side of each sausage link lightly with a fork or tip of a sharp knife to release some of the juices. Remove the sausage links from the pan and place on a cutting board. Let them cool slightly, then slice each sausage link on an angle into 3 to 4 pieces. Transfer them back into the frying pan with all the accumulated juices.

3. In a small bowl, mix together the salt, pepper, garlic powder, onion powder, basil, paprika, Italian seasoning and red pepper flakes. Then set the seasoning mixture aside.

4. In a large bowl, add the sliced mini sweet peppers, sliced bell peppers, and red and yellow onions. Pierce each potato with a fork and put them in the bowl. Add 2 tbsp. olive oil and about ⅓ of the seasoning mixture. Add the sliced sausage pieces with all the juices into the bowl and mix together until all the vegetables and sausage are combined and coated with the olive oil, juices and seasoning mixture. Then transfer to a large 16 inch roasting pan.

5. Place the chicken thighs on a cutting board and cut two small slices on the top skin side of each thigh. Drizzle olive oil and sprinkle seasoning mixture on each thigh. Then place them in the roasting pan, spacing them evenly around the vegetables. Sprinkle the remainder of the seasoning mixture and a little more ground black pepper on top of the chicken and vegetables.

6. Place in the oven and bake uncovered for 45 minutes. Then baste the chicken and vegetables with juices in the roasting pan and sprinkle with fresh thyme. Bake for an additional 20 minutes, or until vegetables are caramelized and the chicken is fully cooked and browned. Sprinkle with chopped fresh parsley and serve.

ONE PAN CHEESY CHICKEN AND RICE

Prep. time: 15 min | Total time: 30min | Serves: 4

INGREDIENTS:

- 1 Lb. Chicken Strips (cut into bite size pieces)
- 2 Tbsp. Butter
- 2 Tbsp. Olive Oil
- 1 Tsp. Minced Garlic
- 1 Cup Diced Yellow Onion
- 2¼ Cups Chicken Broth
- 1 Can Condensed Cream of Mushroom Soup
- 1 Bag Frozen Mixed Vegetables (thawed)
- 2 Cups Shredded Sharp Cheddar Cheese (divided)
- 1 Cup Uncooked Rice
- 1 Tsp. Salt
- 1 Tsp. Pepper
- 2 Tbsp. Parsley (Fresh or dried)

DIRECTIONS:

1. In a skillet on medium heat, add olive oil and butter. Once the butter has melted, add the diced onion and sauté until tender.
2. Add the chicken and season with salt and pepper. Partially cook the chicken for about 3 to 4 minutes, then add the garlic and cook for another minute.
3. Move the chicken mixture to one side of the pan and add one cup of uncooked rice to the other side. Toast the rice until it turns golden brown.
4. Then turn the heat down to medium-low and stir in the chicken broth. Cover and let simmer for 18 to 20 minutes.
5. Once the rice is cooked, stir in the cream of mushroom soup, mixed vegetables, and 1 cup of the shredded sharp cheddar cheese.
6. Reduce heat to low, cover and cook for about 5 more minutes. Turn the heat off and top with the remaining shredded sharp cheddar cheese and parsley. Cover for about 2 minutes, or until the cheese has melted and serve.

WHITE CHICKEN ENCHILADAS

Prep. time: 15 min   Total time: 30 min   Serves: 6

INGREDIENTS:

- 1 Rotisserie Chicken (2 cups shredded)
- 1 Cup Diced Yellow Onions
- ½ Jar (8oz.) Medium White Queso Cheese Dip
- ½ Block (4oz.) Cream Cheese (softened)
- 3 Cups Shredded Mexican Blend Cheese (divided)
- Flour Tortillas (medium soft taco size)
- ½ Cup Chopped Green Onions

White Sauce Ingredients:

- 6 Tbsp. Butter
- 6 Tbsp. All-Purpose Flour
- 3 Cups Chicken Broth
- ½ Cup Heavy Cream
- ½ Jar (8oz.) Medium White Queso Cheese Dip
- 1 Tsp. Garlic Powder
- 1 Tsp. Salt
- 2 Cups Sour Cream
- 1 - 2 4oz. Cans Diced Mild Green Chiles

DIRECTIONS:

1. Preheat oven to 350 degrees. Spray a 9 x 13 baking dish with nonstick cooking spray.
2. In a bowl, combine softened cream cheese and ½ jar (8oz.) of the white Queso cheese dip (reserve the remaining ½ jar of Queso cheese dip for the white sauce). Mix in the shredded chicken, diced onions, and 1 cup shredded Mexican blend cheese.
3. Fill each tortilla with the chicken mixture and roll. Then place them seam side down, side by side in the baking dish.
4. In a skillet on medium heat, add butter. Once the butter has melted, whisk in flour and cook the flour, whisking constantly, for about 1 - 2 minutes. Then slowly stir in the chicken broth, heavy cream, and the remaining ½ jar (8oz.) of white Queso cheese dip. Season with salt, and garlic powder and continue to stir and cook until the sauce thickens.
5. Remove the skillet from the heat and let the white sauce cool for about 3 minutes. Then add the green chiles and sour cream (if the sauce is too hot, the sour cream may curdle) and stir until the sauce is smooth and creamy.
6. Pour the white sauce over the enchiladas and top with 1 to 2 cups shredded Mexican blend cheese, and chopped green onions. Bake uncovered in the oven for about 20 to 25 minutes, or until the sauce is bubbly and cheese is melted. Serve these delicious enchiladas with Spanish rice, refried beans, and salsa and enjoy!

SOUTHERN SMOTHERED PORK CHOPS

Prep. time: 15 min | Total time: 2.5 hours | Serves: 4

INGREDIENTS:

- 4 Thick Bone-In Center Cut Pork Chops (about 1½-inch thick)
- 2 Tsp. Kosher Salt
- ½ Tsp. Pepper
- ½ Tsp. Paprika
- 1 Tsp. Garlic Powder
- ¾ Cup All-Purpose Flour
- 3 Tbsp. Olive Oil
- 5 Tbsp. Butter (divided)
- 1 Large Sweet Onion (sliced)
- 2 Tbsp. Minced Garlic
- 1 Tbsp. Worcestershire Sauce
- 3½ Cups Chicken Broth

DIRECTIONS:

1. Preheat oven to 350 degrees.
2. Season both sides of the pork chops with salt, pepper, paprika, and garlic powder. In a shallow dish, add flour and season with salt and pepper. Dredge both sides of each pork chop in the flour (reserve about 3 tbsp. of flour for the roux).
3. In a large deep oven-safe frying pan or a cast iron skillet on medium heat, add olive oil and 3 tbsp. butter. Once the butter has melted, place pork chops in the pan and sear both sides until golden brown (about 5 minutes on each side). Then transfer the pork chops to a plate and set aside.
4. Add onions into the same frying pan and sauté about 4 to 5 minutes, then add 2 tbsp. butter. Once the butter has melted, add the minced garlic and sauté the onions and garlic for another couple of minutes. Stir in 3 tbsp. flour and cook for about 4 to 5 minutes until the flour is golden brown (stirring continuously). Whisk in chicken broth and Worcestershire sauce and let simmer for a couple of minutes.
5. Place the pork chops back into the frying pan with the onion gravy. Use a large spoon to coat the pork chops with the gravy. Then cover with a lid or aluminum foil and bake in the oven for about 2 hours, or until the pork chops are fall apart tender.
6. Serve the pork chops smothered in the delicious onion gravy with creamy mashed potatoes, and greens....and enjoy.

BAKED EGGPLANT PARMESAN

INGREDIENTS:

- 2 Medium Eggplants
- 4 Eggs
- 4 Cups Italian Seasoned Breadcrumbs
- 1 24oz. Jar Marinara Sauce (divided)
- 3 Cups Shredded Mozzarella Cheese (divided)
- 2 Cups Shredded Parmesan Cheese (divided)
- 2 Roma Tomatoes (sliced)
- Olive Oil
- Chopped Fresh Basil
- Salt and Pepper

Prep. time:
15 min

Total time:
40 min

Serves: 6

DIRECTIONS:

1. Preheat oven to 400 degrees.

2. Cut each eggplant into 6 round slices (total of 12 slices about ¼-inch thick). Sprinkle salt on both sides of the eggplant slices and place them in a colander. Set a heavy plate on top of the eggplant slices and place the colander in a large bowl. Set aside for about 1 hour to release the juices from the eggplant. Then rinse them well with water and blot dry with paper towels.

3. In a shallow dish, add eggs and whisk together well. In a separate shallow dish, add the Italian seasoned breadcrumbs. Dip each slice of eggplant into the beaten eggs, then dredge in the breadcrumbs. Place them on a baking sheet sprayed with nonstick cooking spray. Bake uncovered in the oven for 10 minutes, then turn the slices over and continue to bake for another 10 minutes until golden brown.

4. Pour half of the jar of marinara sauce into a 9 x 13 baking dish sprayed with nonstick cooking spray. Place 6 eggplant slices in a single layer on top of the sauce. Then put a couple of spoonfuls of marinara sauce on each of the eggplant slices and sprinkle each slice with some of the shredded mozzarella and parmesan cheese and fresh basil. Then put another layer of the eggplant slices, and top with the remaining marinara sauce, and the remaining mozzarella and parmesan cheese. In a shallow dish, drizzle a little olive oil on the sliced Roma tomatoes and season with salt and pepper. Then place them around the eggplant parmesan in the baking dish.

5. Bake uncovered in the oven for 25 minutes, or until sauce is bubbly and cheese is melted and light golden brown. Garnish with fresh basil, then serve and enjoy!

SWEET AND SOUR PORK

INGREDIENTS:

- 1 Lb. Pork Tenderloin (cut into bite size pieces)
- 1 20oz. Can Pineapple Slices in Pineapple Juice (cut into bite size pieces and reserve the juice)
- 1 Tbsp. Soy Sauce
- ¼ Tsp. Salt
- ¼ Tsp Baking Soda
- 3 Eggs
- 2 Cups All-Purpose Flour
- 1 Cup Cornstarch
- Vegetable Oil (for frying)
- Garnish with Sesame Seeds

Prep. time: 4.5 hours | Total time: 30 min | Serves: 4

Sauce Ingredients:

- ½ Cup Ketchup
- ½ Cup Rice Vinegar
- ¼ Cup Granulated Sugar
- ¼ Cup Brown Sugar
- 1 Tsp. Dark Soy Sauce (or 2 tsp. Regular Soy Sauce)
- 1 Tbsp. Duck Sauce
- Reserved Pineapple Juice (divided)
- 1 Tbsp. Cornstarch + 2 Tbsp. Water

Stir Fry Vegetables:

- 2 Tbsp. Vegetable Oil
- ½ Cup Sweet Onion (chopped)
- ½ Cup Carrots (sliced thin)
- 1 Green Bell Pepper (cut into bite size pieces)
- 1 Red Bell Pepper (cut into bite size pieces)

DIRECTIONS:

1. Cut a pork tenderloin into 1-inch bite size pieces and place into a bowl. Add soy sauce, salt, baking soda, and 3 tbsp. of pineapple juice (reserve the rest of the pineapple juice for the sauce). Mix together well, cover and place in the refrigerator to marinate for 2 to 4 hours. Then remove the bowl of marinated pork from the refrigerator and set aside while you make the sweet and sour sauce.

2. In a saucepan on medium heat, add ketchup, rice vinegar, granulated sugar, brown sugar, soy sauce, duck sauce, and the reserved pineapple juice. Stir and bring to a simmer. In a small bowl, mix together 1 tbsp. cornstarch and 2 tbsp. water to make a slurry. Then slowly add the cornstarch slurry into the sauce and continue to simmer and stir until the sauce thickens. Then remove it from the heat and set aside.

3. Prepare the wet and dry dredge ingredients for your pieces of pork. In a small bowl, add 3 eggs and whisk together. In a separate bowl, add 2 cups all-purpose flour and 1 cup cornstarch and mix together well. Dip the pieces of pork in the egg, then dredge them in the flour and cornstarch mixture. Repeat this coating process twice.

4. In a deep frying pan, add about 2 inches of vegetable oil and heat to 350 degrees. Fry small batches of the pork (about 7 or 8 pieces at a time) for about 6 minutes, or until golden brown and internal temperature reaches 145 degrees. Then place them on a plate lined with paper towels and set aside.

5. In a hot wok or large skillet, add 2 tbsp. vegetable oil. Once the oil is hot, add onions and carrots and stir-fry for 3 to 4 minutes. Add in the green and red bell peppers and continue to stir-fry for another 3 to 4 minutes. Then add in the pineapple pieces and stir-fry for about 1 minute. Pour the sweet and sour sauce into the wok and add in the pieces of fried pork. Stir it all together until the pork is coated with the sauce and let simmer for a couple of minutes.

6. Serve over a bed of rice and sprinkle on some sesame seeds!

STEVE'S LOW COUNTRY BOIL

Prep. time: 10 min | Total time: 30 min | Serves: 4-6

INGREDIENTS:

- 1 Lb. Raw Shrimp (shell-on)
- 1 Lb. Andouille Cajun Smoked Sausage (cut into 1-inch pieces)
- 1 Large Sweet Onion (cut into large chunks)
- 3 Lemons
- 1 Cup Seafood Seasoning (divided)
- 10 Small Red and Gold Potatoes
- 4 Fresh Sweet Corn on the Cob (cut into 3 pieces)
- 10 White Button Mushrooms
- 1 Stick Butter (melted)

"You gotta try this recipe...the shrimp is so delicious and tender, and the mushrooms are like little flavor bombs!"- Steve Hall

DIRECTIONS:

1. Fill a large stock pot about 2/3 full of water and bring to a boil. Add ½ cup of the seafood seasoning, the chunks of onion, and the juice from 2 small lemons.
2. Then add the small red and gold potatoes and boil for 10 minutes. Add the pieces of sweet corn and boil for 10 more minutes, then the pieces of Andouille sausage and button mushrooms and continue to boil for an additional 10 more minutes.
3. In a separate pot of boiling water, add ¼ cup of the seafood seasoning and the shrimp with shell-on. Bring to a simmer and cook the shrimp for 2 ½ to 3 minutes, or just until the shrimp turns pink. Then remove with a slotted spoon and place on a plate.
4. Using a large slotted spoon, scoop all of the potatoes, corn on the cob, mushrooms, and sausage out of the large stock pot and place them on a large serving platter, or just on a table covered in a bed of newspapers. Then add the cooked shrimp on top, and sprinkle on a light dusting of seafood seasoning over everything.Now squeeze some fresh lemon over the shrimp and serve with melted butter....Delicious!

MAMA MARGE'S SWEET POTATOES AND DUMPLINGS

INGREDIENTS:

Sweet Potatoes:
- 3 Medium Sweet Potatoes (peeled and quartered)
- 1 Stick Butter
- 1 Tbsp. Cinnamon
- 1 Tsp. Nutmeg
- 1 Cup Sugar

Dumplings:
- 2½ Cups Self-Rising Flour
- 1 Cup Milk
- ¼ Cup Vegetable Oil

Prep. time: 10 min

Total time:
40 min

Serves: 4

DIRECTIONS:

1. Place sweet potatoes in a Dutch oven and fill with ¾ full of water. Cover and bring to a boil for about 25 minutes, or until sweet potatoes are tender. Prepare the dumplings while the sweet potatoes are cooking.

2. In a bowl, add flour, milk, and vegetable oil. Stir together until well blended and the dumpling mixture forms into a thick batter. Then set aside.

3. Once the sweet potatoes are tender, add butter, cinnamon, nutmeg, and sugar. Stir until butter has melted. Then gently drop the dumpling batter by spoonfuls into the Dutch oven with the sweet potatoes (do not stir). Continue to boil for about 10 to 15 minutes and gently turn the dumplings while they are cooking. Then remove from heat, and cover and let dumplings finish cooking and cool a little.

4. Spoon the sweet potatoes with the dumplings into a bowl, serve and enjoy.

SOUTHERN FRIED CABBAGE WITH SAUSAGE AND BACON

Prep. time: 15 min | Total time: 20 min | Serves: 4-5

INGREDIENTS:

- 1 Head Green Cabbage (roughly chopped)
- 1 Lb. Bacon (cut into 1-inch pieces)
- 1 Lb. Smoked Sausage (sliced into ¼-inch round pieces)
- 1 Cup Red Bell Pepper (diced)
- 1 Cup Green Bell Pepper (diced)
- 1 Cup Sweet Onion (diced)
- 1 Tsp. Ground Pepper
- 1 Tsp. Salt
- 1 Tsp. Cajun Seasoning
- 2 Tsp. Garlic Powder
- 1 Tsp. Onion Powder
- 2 Tbsp. Butter

DIRECTIONS:

1. In a large Dutch oven or large deep skillet on medium heat, add bacon and cook until crispy. Remove with a slotted spoon, place on a plate and set aside.
2. In the bacon drippings, add the sliced smoked sausage and cook for about 2 to 3 minutes until lightly browned. Remove sausage with a slotted spoon and place on the plate with the bacon and set aside.
3. Add the diced onion and green and red bell peppers in the bacon drippings along with butter and sauté until soft. Add half of the chopped cabbage and stir into the onion and peppers. Cover for 2 to 3 minutes, then stir in the remaining cabbage. Cover and continue to cook for another 10 minutes, or until the cabbage is tender (stirring occasionally).
4. Season the cabbage with salt, pepper, onion powder, garlic powder, and Cajun seasoning. Stir until the cabbage is coated with the seasonings. Then add the sausage and bacon back into the pot with the cabbage and toss to combine.
5. Serve this delicious southern dish along with some cornbread and enjoy!

PASTA DISHES

PASTA CARBONARA WITH BACON

Prep. time: 15 min | Total time: 20 min | Serves: 4

INGREDIENTS:

- 1 Lb. Spaghetti Pasta
- 1 Tbsp. Salt
- 1 Lb. Thick Cut Bacon or Pancetta (chopped)
- 1 Tbsp. Minced Garlic
- 4 Egg Yolks (room temperature)
- 2 Whole Eggs (room temperature)
- 2-3 Tbsp. Half and Half
- 1½ Cups Grated Romano Parmesan Blend Cheese (divided)
- ½ Tsp. Ground Black Pepper
- 2 Tbsp. Fresh Parsley (chopped)

DIRECTIONS:

1. In a medium bowl, whisk together the eggs, half and half, 1 cup grated Romano Parmesan blend cheese, and black pepper. Then set aside.

2. In a large skillet on medium heat, add the bacon and cook until brown and crispy. Turn the heat to low, add the minced garlic and cook for another 1, then remove the skillet from the heat.

3. While the bacon is cooking, fill a large pot with water and bring to a boil. Then add salt and the spaghetti pasta and cook (stirring frequently) until al dente or firm. Reserve 1 cup of the starchy pasta water and set aside. Then drain the spaghetti (do not rinse).

4. Add the hot spaghetti into the skillet with the bacon, garlic, and bacon grease, and gently toss together with tongs until well combined.

5. Then pour the egg mixture over the hot spaghetti and toss together until the spaghetti is coated with the mixture (the hot spaghetti will cook the egg mixture, so no need to put it back on the heat). Add starchy pasta water a little at a time to thin the carbonara sauce until desired creamy consistency is reached.

6. Serve and garnish with more of the grated Romano Parmesan blend cheese, fresh parsley and black pepper. So easy and delicious!

STUFFED PASTA SHELLS AND SAUSAGE

INGREDIENTS:

- 1 Box Jumbo Pasta Shells (about 16 shells)
- 1 Lb. Mild Italian Sausage Links
- 4 Cups Marinara Sauce
- 1 Medium Sweet Onion (chopped)
- 1 Cup Spinach (chopped)
- 1 12oz. Tub Ricotta Cheese
- 1 Tbsp. Minced Garlic
- 1 Cup Shredded Mozzarella Cheese
- 1 Cup Grated Romano Parmesan Cheese (divided)
- 4oz. of Cream Cheese (softened)
- 2 Eggs (lightly beaten)
- 2 Tbsp. Fresh Parsley (finely chopped)
- ½ Tsp. Basil
- 1 Tsp. Salt
- Olive Oil
- Nonstick Cooking Spray

Prep. time: 15 min | Total time: 50 min | Serves: 5-6

DIRECTIONS:

1. Preheat oven to 350 degrees.
2. Bring a large pot of water to a boil on medium heat. Then add the jumbo pasta shells and 1 tsp. of salt, and boil uncovered (stirring occasionally) until al dente. Drain and rinse the pasta shells in cold water and place them on a baking sheet lined with parchment paper to finish cooling.
3. In a skillet on medium heat, add a little olive oil and the Italian sausage links. Brown the Italian sausage on one side, then turn the links over and pierce them with a fork. Continue cooking them until the other side is browned, but not fully cooked. Transfer them to a plate, and set aside.
4. In the same skillet, sauté the onions in the sausage drippings until tender, then add the spinach and sauté until it wilts. Remove from heat and set aside.
5. In a large bowl, add ricotta cheese, sautéed onions and spinach, ½ cup Romano Parmesan cheese, cream cheese, eggs, parsley, and minced garlic. Stir until well combined.
6. In a 9 x 13 casserole dish sprayed with nonstick cooking spray (or greased with some olive oil), add several spoonful's of the marinara sauce and spread it evenly (just enough to lightly coat the bottom of the baking dish).
7. Spoon the ricotta cheese mixture into the pasta shells and place them in the baking dish along with the partially cooked Italian sausage links (sliced in half). Then pour the remaining marinara sauce evenly over the stuffed pasta shells and sausage. Top with the mozzarella cheese, sprinkle with ½ cup Romano Parmesan grated cheese, and fresh chopped basil.
8. Cover with parchment paper (to keep the cheese from sticking), then foil, and bake in the oven for 30 minutes. Then remove the foil and parchment paper and continue to bake an additional 10 to 15 minutes, or until the cheese is melted.

ONE POT CHEESY TACO PASTA

Prep. time: 10 min | Total time: 20 min | Serves: 4

INGREDIENTS:

- 1 Lb. Lean Ground Beef
- 1 Medium Sweet Onion (diced)
- 1 Tbsp. Minced Garlic
- 1 Packet Taco Seasoning Mix
- 1 Can Diced Tomatoes and Green Chilies
- 1 15oz. Can Tomato Sauce
- 1 15oz. Can Sweet Corn (drained)
- 1 Cup Shredded Cheddar Cheese (divided)
- 2 Cups Uncooked Pasta Shells (medium size)
- 2-3 Cups Water
- 1 Cup Shredded Mexican Blend Cheese
- Sour Cream
- ¼ Cup Chopped Fresh Green Onions
- Salt and Pepper to taste

DIRECTIONS:

1. In a deep skillet or large pot on medium heat, add the ground beef and diced sweet onions. Cook until the ground beef is browned. Then add the minced garlic and season the beef with ½ of the taco seasoning packet and cook for another 1 to 2 minutes.

2. Add diced tomatoes and green chilies, tomato sauce, and sweet corn. Bring to a simmer and add the remaining ½ taco seasoning packet and stir in ½ cup of the shredded cheddar cheese.

3. Add 2½ cups of water and the uncooked pasta shells (you may need a little more water depending on the size of the pasta shells). Reduce heat to low, cover and simmer for 10 to 15 minutes, or until pasta is al dente (stirring occasionally).

4. Then remove from heat, and top with the shredded Mexican blend cheese, remaining ½ cup of shredded cheddar cheese, and green onions. Cover to let the cheese melt.

5. Serve and garnish with sour cream and enjoy this delicious easy, cheesy, one pot pasta dish!

GARLIC BUTTER SHRIMP SCAMPI

Prep. time: 10 min

Total time: 20 min

Serves: 4

INGREDIENTS:

- 1½ Pounds Raw Shrimp (Peeled, Deveined, and Tail Off)
- 4 Tbsp. Olive Oil (divided)
- 2 Tsp. Salt (divided)
- 1 Tsp. Pepper
- 1 Stick Salted Butter + 2 Tbsp. (divided)
- 3 Tbsp. Minced Garlic
- 1-2 Green Onions (finely chopped)
- 1 Cup Dry White Wine
- ½ Tsp. Red Pepper Flakes
- 1 16oz. Pkg. Spaghetti or Pasta of your choice

Garnish:

- Grated Parmesan Cheese
- Fresh Chopped Parsley
- Fresh Lemon Juice

DIRECTIONS:

1. Bring a large pot of water to a boil on medium heat. Add spaghetti and 1 tsp. of salt and cook until the pasta is al dente. Drain the spaghetti, then add 2 tbsp. of olive oil and toss until well coated. Then set aside.

2. In a large bowl, drizzle olive oil on both sides of the shrimp and season with salt and pepper.

3. In a large skillet on medium-high heat, melt 2 tbsp. of butter. Then add the shrimp and cook on both sides just until they turn pink (about 3 minutes). Remove shrimp with a slotted spoon from the pan and place on a plate and set aside.

4. In the same skillet on medium heat, add 1 stick of butter. Once the butter has melted, add minced garlic and sauté for about 1 minute until the garlic is fragrant, then add green onions and continue to sauté for another minute. Pour in the white wine, and add the red pepper flakes. Reduce heat to medium-low and simmer for about 3 to 4 minutes, or until the wine reduces by about half. Add the cooked shrimp back into the skillet and let simmer for another minute, then remove from heat.

5. Pour the garlic butter sauce and shrimp over the spaghetti. Serve and garnish with grated parmesan cheese, fresh chopped parsley, and a squeeze of fresh lemon, and enjoy this incredibly delicious classic dish!

EASY BAKED MEXICAN LASAGNA

Prep. time: 10 min | Total time: 40 min

Serves: 6

INGREDIENTS:

- 1 Lb. Lean Ground Beef (85/15)
- 1 20oz. Pkg. Four Cheese Ravioli Refrigerated Pasta
- 1 Yellow Onion (diced)
- 2 Tbsp. Taco Seasoning
- 1 Tsp. Garlic Powder
- 1 Tsp. Onion Powder
- 1 10oz. Can Diced Tomatoes and Green Chilies (drained)
- 1 15oz. Can Sweet Corn (drained)
- 1 19oz. Can Mild Red Enchilada Sauce (divided)
- 1 15oz. Jar White Queso Dip (divided)
- 3½ Cups Shredded Mexican Blend Cheese (divided)
- ½ Cup Chopped Green Onions
- Garnish with Sour Cream and chopped Cilantro

DIRECTIONS:

1. Preheat oven to 375 degrees.

2. In a large skillet on medium heat, add the ground beef and yellow onions, and cook until the beef is browned. Season with the taco seasoning, garlic powder and onion powder. Add the sweet corn and diced tomatoes and green chilies, and continue to cook for 2 to 3 minutes, then remove from the heat and set aside.

3. In a 9 x 13 baking dish sprayed with nonstick cooking spray, add about ¼ cup of the enchilada sauce and spread it thinly on the bottom. Place half of the ravioli in a single layer over the sauce. Then top with all of the meat mixture and spread it evenly with a spoon. Pour ½ of the remaining enchilada sauce over the meat mixture, then ½ of the queso dip, and ½ of the shredded cheese. Finish with a single layer of the ravioli, then top with the rest of the enchilada sauce, queso dip, and shredded cheese. Sprinkle with chopped green onions.

4. Bake uncovered in the oven for 30 to 35 minutes, or until the sauce is bubbly and the cheese is melted, and golden brown. Remove from the oven and let sit for about 10 minutes. Then serve and garnish with a dollop of sour cream and chopped cilantro.

PICKLED

PICKLED WATERMELON RIND

INGREDIENTS:

- 1 Small Watermelon

Brine:

- 1½ Cup of Water
- 1½ Cups Apple Cider or White Vinegar
- 1½ Cups Granulated White Sugar
- 1 Tsp. Whole Black Peppercorns
- ½ Tsp. Red Pepper Flakes
- 3 Tbsp. Kosher Salt
- 1 Tbsp. Pickling Spice
- 2 Tsp. Coriander Seeds

"They are sweet, spicy, crunchy, and so delicious...you gotta try them!" - Steve Hall

DIRECTIONS:

1. Using a heavy sharp knife, cut off both ends of the watermelon, then stand it up on one of the flat ends and cut slices straight down about 2 inches wide. Then cut the red watermelon from each slice leaving about ⅛-inch of it on the rind. Use a vegetable peeler and cut off all the outer green skin from each slice. Then cut each rind slice into ½-inch cubes and put them in sterilized quart or pint glass jars with lids leaving about 1-inch of headspace at the top.

2. In a large pot on medium heat, add all the brine ingredients and stir together well. Continue to stir and bring to a boil, then reduce heat to medium-low and simmer for about 1 minute, or until the sugar is dissolved. Remove from the heat and let it cool for a few minutes.

3. Pour the brine while it is still very warm (not hot) over the cubed watermelon rinds in the glass jars leaving about ½-inch of headspace at the top and cover with the lids (twist the lids on until snug). Turn the jars upside down and place in the refrigerator for 1 to 4 days, then serve and enjoy. They will keep in the refrigerator for about 2 to 3 weeks.

PICKLED HOT DOGS AND ONIONS

INGREDIENTS:

- 2 1 Lb. Packages Hot Dogs
- 2 Small Sweet Onions (sliced)
- 8 Garlic Cloves (peeled and cut in half)

Brine:

- 4 Cups White Vinegar
- ½ Tsp. Salt
- 1 Tsp. Cumin
- 1½ Tbsp. Pickling Spice
- 1 Tsp. Red Pepper Flakes
- 1 Tbsp. Minced Garlic
- 1 Cup Hot Sauce
- ½ - 1 Cup Granulated White Sugar

DIRECTIONS:

1. Cut the hot dogs into bite size pieces. Then put layers of the hot dogs, sliced onions, and garlic cloves into sterilized quart glass jars with lids. Leave about 1-inch of headspace at the top of each jar.

2. In a large saucepan on medium heat, add all the brine ingredients and stir until combined. Continue to stir and bring to a boil, then reduce the heat to medium-low and let it simmer for 3 to 5 minutes, or until the sugar is dissolved. Remove from the heat and let it cool slightly.

3. Pour the hot brine over the hot dogs and onions in the jars and cover with the lids.

4. Place in the refrigerator for 3 days before serving, then enjoy these hot, sweet, and spicy hot dogs and onions!

PICKLED EGGS AND BEETS

INGREDIENTS:

- 8 Eggs (hard boiled and peeled)
- 1 15oz. Can Sliced Beets (with juice)
- ½ Cup Granulated White Sugar
- ½ Cup White Vinegar
- ½ Cup Water
- ½ Tsp. Pickling Spice

DIRECTIONS:

1. Make the Hard Boiled Eggs: Place eggs in a pot in a single layer and cover them completely with cold water. Turn the heat on high and bring to a boil. Let the eggs boil for 1 minute, then remove from the heat and cover the pot. Leave eggs in the hot water for 15 minutes. Then drain and transfer the eggs into a large bowl of ice water. Let them sit in the ice water bath for 15 minutes. Remove the eggs from the ice water, peel them and set aside.

2. Make the Brine: In a saucepan on medium heat, pour the juice from the can of beets into the pot, then add the sugar, vinegar, water, and pickling spice, and stir to combine. Continue to stir and bring to a boil, then reduce the heat to medium-low and let it simmer for 3 minutes, or until the sugar is dissolved.

3. Pour the sliced beets out of the can onto a plate, and cut them in half. Then add the beets into the saucepan with the brine and gently stir and simmer for about 3 minutes. Remove from the heat and cool slightly.

4. In a sterilized quart glass jar, layer the hard boiled eggs and the beets. Then pour the hot brine over them and cover with the lid. Refrigerate for at least 4 hours or overnight, then serve and enjoy!

SWEET PICKLED VEGETABLES

INGREDIENTS:

- Cauliflower (cut into florets)
- Baby Carrots (sliced lengthwise in half)
- Green Bell Pepper (cut into strips)
- Red Bell Pepper (cut into strips)
- Cucumber (skin on/ seeds removed/cut into wedges)
- Green Beans (trim off ends/cut in half)
- Yellow Squash (cut into half moon slices)
- Zucchini (cut into half moon slices)
- Sweet Onions (thinly sliced)
- Asparagus Tips

Brine:
- 4 Cups White Vinegar
- 2 Cups Granulated White Sugar
- 1 Heaping Tbsp. Pickling Spice

DIRECTIONS:

1. Prepare the Vegetables: wash the vegetables well and dry, and cut them up. Then place them in layers into sterilized wide mouth quart glass jars with lids. Leave about ½-inch of headspace at the top of each jar.

2. Make the Brine: In a saucepan on medium heat, add the white vinegar, sugar, and pickling spice. Stir and bring to a boil, then reduce the heat to medium-low, continue to stir and let simmer for 3 to 5 minutes, or until the sugar is dissolved. Remove from the heat and let the brine cool completely.

3. Pour the cool brine over the vegetables in the jars and cover tightly with the lids. Turn the jars upside down and place in the refrigerator for 3 days, then serve and enjoy!

_____

"I could almost drink this stuff straight up...it's that good!" - Steve Hall

_____

WORLD'S BEST PICKLED FISH OR SHRIMP

INGREDIENTS:

- 4 Lbs. Frozen Raw Tilapia Fillets (Boneless/Skinless) (thawed and cut into bite-sized pieces) (-or- 4 Lbs. Frozen Raw Small Shrimp (peeled/deveined/tail-off) (thawed)
- 3 Large Sweet Onions (sliced)
- 1½ Cups Canning & Pickling Salt (no iodine)
- 6 Cups White Vinegar

Brine:
- 8 Cups White Vinegar
- 6 Cups Granulated White Sugar
- ⅓ Cup Pickling Spice
- ¼ Cup White Zinfandel Wine

"They will keep in the refrigerator for about 6 to 8 weeks...if they last that long....they are absolutely delicious!" - Steve Hall

---

DIRECTIONS:

1. In a one gallon jar with a lid, add a layer of the raw fish or shrimp, then a layer of the salt, and repeat the process. Then pour enough white vinegar into the jar to completely cover the fish or shrimp by 2 to 3 inches. Place the jar in the refrigerator for 5 days (shake the jar once every day to mix the salt into the vinegar).

2. After 5 days, remove from the refrigerator, drain and rinse all the salt and vinegar off of the fish or shrimp with cold water (discard all of the vinegar and salt the fish or shrimp was soaking in). Then place the fish or shrimp in a large bowl of fresh cold water and ice cubes for 1 hour.

3. Make the Brine: In a pot on medium heat, add 8 cups white vinegar, sugar, pickling spice, and white Zinfandel wine. Stir and bring to a boil, then reduce the heat to medium-low, continue to stir and let simmer for 3 to 5 minutes, or until the sugar is dissolved. Remove from the heat and let the brine cool completely. Then place in the refrigerator until it is cold.

4. Drain the fish or shrimp. Then in a clean one gallon jar, add a layer of the fish or shrimp, then a layer of the sweet onions, and continue with the layers until the jar is packed full. Pour the cold brine over the fish or shrimp and onions until they are completely covered with it. Then cover the jar with the lid and place in the refrigerator for at least 5 days. The longer they are in there, the better they get.

SALADS AND SIDES

FRIED POTATO CAKES aka POTATO PANCAKES

INGREDIENTS:

- 2 Cups Cold Leftover Mashed Potatoes
- 1 Egg (lightly beaten)
- ¾ Cup Self-Rising Flour
- ¼ Cup Whole Milk
- 1 Tsp. Salt
- 1 Tsp. Pepper
- 1 Tsp. Onion Powder
- Vegetable or Corn Oil for frying

Additional Ingredients you can add:

- 1 Cup Shredded Cheddar Cheese
- Green Onions (finely chopped)
- Cooked Crumbled Bacon or Diced Ham

Prep. time:
15 min

Total time:
15 min

Serves: 6-8

DIRECTIONS:

1. In a bowl mix together the potatoes, egg, flour, and milk. Season with salt, pepper, and onion powder. Add your choice of additional ingredients and stir together until smooth. The potato mixture should be thick enough to form into a patty. If it is too thin and runny, add a little more flour, or if it is too thick, add a little more milk.

2. In a cast iron skillet on medium heat, add a little oil to cover the bottom of the skillet. Form the potato mixture into patties and once the oil is hot, carefully drop the potato patties into the skillet. Fry the potato cakes in small batches until they are golden brown on both sides (about 3 to 4 minutes on each side). Add more oil to the skillet between each batch as needed. Place the fried potato cakes on a plate lined with paper towels.

3. Serve these delicious potato cakes with breakfast, as a side dish, or anytime. Top with some sour cream, ranch dressing, or ketchup, and green onions and enjoy!

MISS SHEILA'S BROCCOLI APPLE SALAD

INGREDIENTS:

- 2 Cups Raw Broccoli Florets (cut into bite-sized pieces)
- 1 Cup Diced Sweet Apples
- ½ Cup Shredded Carrots
- ½ Cup Chopped Red Onion
- ½ Cup Dried Cranberries
- ½ Cup Chopped Pecans

Dressing:

- 1 Cup Greek Yogurt
- 1 Cup Mayonnaise
- ¼ Cup Fresh Lemon Juice
- 1 Tsp. Sugar
- Pinch of Salt and Pepper

DIRECTIONS:

1. In a large bowl, add all the salad ingredients and toss together. Then set aside.
2. In a separate bowl, add all the dressing ingredients and whisk together until creamy and smooth. Add a little bit of water to thin the dressing if it is too thick.
3. Pour the dressing over the salad and toss until well coated. Place in the refrigerator to chill for about 1 hour, then serve and enjoy!

Prep. time: 15 min

Total time: 75 min

Serves: 6-8

CORN SALAD WITH HOMEMADE DRESSING

INGREDIENTS:

- 3 Cans Sweet Corn (drained)
- 1 Lb. Grape or Cherry Tomatoes (halved)
- 1 English Cucumber (diced)
- 1 Red Onion (finely chopped)
- 1 Red Bell Pepper (chopped)
- 1 12oz. Jar Marinated Artichoke Hearts
- ½ Cup Fresh Basil Leaves (chopped)

Dressing:

- ¼ Cup Extra Virgin Olive Oil
- 2 - 3 Tbsp. Balsamic Vinegar
- 1 - 2 Tbsp. Lemon Juice (freshly squeezed)
- 1 Tsp. Garlic Powder
- ½ Tsp. Salt
- ½ Tsp. Freshly Ground Black Pepper
- 1 Tsp. Sugar (optional)

Toppings:

- 1 Large Avocado (peeled, pitted, sliced in wedges)
- Drizzle Fresh Lemon Juice on the Avocado
- ¼ Cup Fresh Parsley Leaves (chopped)
- Salt and Ground Black Pepper to taste

DIRECTIONS:

1. In a large bowl, add all the salad ingredients and toss to combine. Then set aside.
2. In a small mixing bowl, whisk together all the dressing ingredients. Then pour over the salad and toss until well coated. Place the salad in the refrigerator to chill for about 30 minutes. Then remove from the refrigerator and toss again.
3. Top with slices of avocado, fresh parsley, and season with salt and pepper. Serve and enjoy this delicious side salad for any occasion.

 Prep. time: 15 min

 Total time: 30 min

 Serves: 6-8

DEEP-FRIED CORN ON THE COB

INGREDIENTS:

- 8 Ears Frozen Sweet Corn on the Cob (thawed)
- 2 Cups Whole Buttermilk
- 2 Cups Fish Breading Mix (-or-) 2 Cups All-Purpose Flour
- 1 Tsp. Salt
- ½ Tsp. Pepper
- 1 Tsp. Onion Powder
- 1 Tsp. Garlic Powder
- Creole Seasoning
- Vegetable Oil for frying

Prep. time:
15 min

Total time:
20 min

Serves: 6-8

DIRECTIONS:

1. Pour the buttermilk into a shallow bowl. In a separate shallow bowl, add 2 cups of the fish breading mix, or add 2 cups of the all-purpose flour, salt, pepper, onion powder, and garlic powder and whisk together.

2. Dip each ear of sweet corn in the buttermilk and shake off most of the excess. Then roll each one in the fish breading mix, or seasoned flour mixture. Sprinkle each ear of corn with a light dusting of the Creole seasoning, then place them on a baking sheet and let sit for about 10 minutes before deep frying.

3. In a deep fryer, add vegetable oil and heat to 350 degrees. Place the ears of corn into the deep fryer and cook for 5 to 7 minutes, or until golden brown. Then place them on a baking sheet lined with paper towels and let cool for a few minutes before serving.

WILD GAME

VENISON POT PIE

INGREDIENTS:

- 1 Pint Jar of Canned Venison (drained)
- 2 12oz. Jars Brown Gravy
- 2 Tbsp. Dried Minced Onions
- ½ Cup Frozen Peas (thawed)
- ½ Cup Frozen Carrots (thawed)
- ¼ Cup Frozen Sweet Corn (thawed)
- 1 15oz. Can White Potatoes (drained)
- ¼ Tsp. Salt
- ½ Tsp. Pepper
- 1 Frozen Deep Dish Pie Crust
- 1 Box Refrigerated Pie Crust
- 1 Egg
- 1 Tsp. Milk

Prep. time:
15 min

Total time:
50 min

Serves: 4

DIRECTIONS:

1. Preheat oven to 375 degrees. Set the frozen deep dish pie crust and 1 roll of the refrigerated pie crust out at room temperature for about 15 minutes before filling and baking.
2. In a large bowl, add the canned venison meat. Then stir in the brown gravy, minced onions, peas, carrots, and corn. Season with salt and pepper.
3. Cut the canned potatoes into ½ inch cubes, then add them into the meat mixture.
4. Pour the meat mixture into the deep dish pie crust. Then unroll 1 softened refrigerated pie crust and place on top of the meat mixture. Trim any excess pie crust, then crimp or flute the edges together to seal.
5. In a small bowl, whisk together the egg and milk. Then using a basting brush, lightly brush the pie crust with the egg wash. Cut 4 small slits on the top of the pie crust to create steam vents.
6. Bake in the oven for 20 to 25 minutes, or until golden brown. Remove from the oven and let sit for about 10 minutes, then serve and enjoy!

OUTSTANDING VENISON STROGANOFF

INGREDIENTS:

- 2 Pint Jars of Canned Venison (reserve juice)
- 2 Tbsp. Vegetable Oil
- 1 Cup Chopped Sweet Onions
- 2 Tbsp. All-Purpose Flour
- 1 Tbsp. Brown Sugar
- 2 Cups Mushrooms (quartered)
- 2 Tbsp. Minced Garlic
- ¼ Cup Heavy Whipping Cream
- ½ Cup Cream of Mushroom Soup
- ½ Cup Tomato Paste
- 1 Cup Sour Cream
- ½ Tsp. Salt
- ½ Tsp. Pepper
- 1 Tsp. Paprika
- 1 16oz. Package Egg Noodles

Prep. time: 15 min

Total time: 20 min

Serves: 4

DIRECTIONS:

1. In a skillet on medium heat, add vegetable oil and onions. Sauté the onions for 3 to 4 minutes, then add the flour and cook for another 2 minutes.

2. Add in the brown sugar, mushrooms, garlic, heavy cream, cream of mushroom soup, and the reserved juice from 1 of the pint jars of canned venison. Cook for 3 to 4 minutes, or until the mushrooms are tender. Then stir in the tomato paste and sour cream. Add a little more of the reserved venison juice if the sauce is too thick.

3. Add the canned venison meat and gently stir it into the sauce mixture. Season with salt, pepper, and paprika. Reduce heat to medium-low, cover and simmer for about 5 minutes while cooking the egg noodles.

4. Cook the egg noodles until al dente according to package directions and drain.

5. Serve this delicious Venison Stroganoff over a bed of the egg noodles and enjoy!

FRIED MOOSE HEART

INGREDIENTS:

- 1 Moose Heart
- 5 Eggs
- ¼ Tsp. Salt
- ½ Tsp. Pepper
- ½ Tsp. Onion Powder
- ½ Tsp. Garlic Powder
- 2 Cups Butter Crackers (crushed)
- 1 Stick Butter
- 2 Tbsp. Vegetable Oil

Prep. time:
15 min

Total time:
20 min

Serves: 4

DIRECTIONS:

1. Preparing the moose heart: make sure it has already been rinsed and purged, and all the fat, valves, and tubes have been trimmed away. Then cut the heart in half lengthwise, and trim out everything that doesn't look like red meat. Slice the moose heart into steaks about ⅜-inch thick against the grain.
2. In a bowl, whisk together the eggs, salt, pepper, onion powder, and garlic powder. Pour the egg mixture in a shallow dish.
3. In a separate shallow dish, add the crushed butter crackers.
4. Dip each moose heart steak into the egg mixture. Then press into the butter crackers, making sure both sides are covered.
5. In a skillet on medium-high heat, add vegetable oil and butter. Once the vegetable oil is hot and the butter has melted, fry the moose heart steaks until golden brown on both sides.
6. Place on a plate lined with paper towels and let rest for 5 minutes, then serve.

VENISON HAMBURGER SOUP

INGREDIENTS:

- 3 Lbs. Ground Venison
- 2 Tbsp. Olive Oil
- 1 Tsp. Salt
- 1 Tsp. Pepper
- 1 15oz. Can Sweet Peas
- 1 15oz. Can Sweet Corn
- 1 15oz. Can Green Beans
- 1 15oz. Can Sliced Carrots
- 1 10oz. Can Diced Tomatoes and Green Chilies
- 1 15oz. Can Diced Tomatoes
- 1 24oz. Jar Spaghetti Sauce
- 3 Cups Water
- 1 Large Sweet Onion (diced)
- 2 Tbsp. Butter (melted)
- 1 Tbsp. Garlic Powder
- ¼ Cup White Zinfandel Wine (optional)
- Salt and Pepper to taste

Prep. time: 15 min

Total time: 45 min

Serves: 4

DIRECTIONS:

1. In a large cast iron skillet on medium heat, add the olive oil and ground venison. Cook the venison until browned (breaking it up into chunks while browning). Then season with salt and pepper.

2. In an 8 quart stock pot on medium heat, add the browned venison. Then add all the cans of vegetables with juice, spaghetti sauce, water, onions, butter, garlic powder, and white Zinfandel wine and stir to combine.

3. Bring the soup just to a boil, then reduce heat to medium-low, partially cover and let simmer for 30 minutes. Season with salt and pepper to taste and garnish with Jalapeño peppers. Serve with crackers and enjoy!

BAKED RABBIT STEW

Prep. time: 20 min

Total time: 4-5 hours

Serves: 4

INGREDIENTS:

- 1 Whole Rabbit
- 2 Cups All-Purpose Flour
- 1 Tsp. Salt
- 1 Tsp. Pepper
- 1 Tsp. Garlic Powder
- 1 Tsp. Onion Powder
- Vegetable Oil for frying
- 2 Cans Cream of Mushroom Soup
- 1 32oz. Box Chicken Broth
- ½ Stick Butter (melted)
- ½ Tsp. Salt
- ½ Tsp. Pepper
- 1 Quart Half and Half (slightly warmed)
- 1 Tbsp. Minced Garlic
- 1 Cup Carrots (chopped)
- 1 Large Sweet Onion (chopped)
- 2 Cups Mushrooms (sliced)
- 1 Bag Frozen Pepper and Onion Stir-Fry Veggies (sliced green, red & yellow peppers & onions)
- 10 Petite Gold Potatoes (quartered)
- Salt and Pepper to taste

DIRECTIONS:

1. Preheat oven to 205 degrees.
2. Cut the rabbit with poultry shears into 8 pieces, and cut the belly flap into about 4 pieces. In a shallow bowl, whisk together the flour, salt, pepper, garlic powder, and onion powder. Then dredge each piece of rabbit in the flour mixture.
3. In a cast iron skillet on medium heat, add ½-inch of vegetable oil and heat to 350 degrees. Fry each piece of rabbit until golden brown on both sides (only fry a few pieces at a time so the skillet is not overcrowded, and check the oil temperature between each batch). Then place each piece into a large Dutch oven.
4. In a large bowl, add the cream of mushroom soup, chicken broth, melted butter, salt, and pepper and stir until combined. Then pour the soup mixture over the rabbit in the Dutch oven. Place the Dutch oven on the stovetop on medium heat and bring just to a simmer. Once it comes to a simmer, place in the oven, cover and bake at 205 degrees for 3 to 4 hours.
5. Remove from the oven and add the half and half (slightly warm in the microwave before adding), minced garlic, carrots, onions, mushrooms, stir-fry vegetables, and potatoes. Then cover and place it back in the oven at 205 degrees for about 1 more hour. Season with salt and pepper to taste and serve the most delicious stew you've ever had!

"If I had to pick one recipe as my final meal, it would be this Rabbit Stew!"
Steve Hall
Note: This was the last recipe Steve filmed before he passed away in Dec 2018. Rest in Peace Steve Hall.

DESSERTS

GRANDMA'S CREAM PUFFS

INGREDIENTS:

- 1 Cup Water
- 1 Stick Butter
- ½ Tsp. Salt
- 1 Cup All-Purpose Flour
- 4 Eggs (room temperature)
- 1 Box Instant Vanilla Pudding
- 3 Cups Whole Milk
- 1 Tub Cool Whip (divided)
- ½ Cup Powdered Confectioners Sugar

Jennifer & Momma Donna

Prep. time:
10 min

Total time:
45 min

Serves: 8

DIRECTIONS:

1. Preheat oven to 400 degrees.

2. In a saucepan on medium-high heat, add water, butter, and salt and bring to a boil. Remove from heat and stir in flour until well combined and it forms into a ball. Transfer to a mixing bowl and let cool. Then add eggs one at a time and mix well after each egg. The pastry dough should be smooth and shiny. Let sit and cool for about 10 minutes, or until the dough has a consistency like thick creamy peanut butter. Drop by heaping teaspoons onto a baking sheet lined with parchment paper. Bake at 400 degrees for 5 minutes, then reduce heat to 350 degrees and bake for 30 minutes. Remove from the oven and let cool completely before filling.

3. In a medium bowl, whisk together the instant vanilla pudding and milk for about 2 minutes, or until it thickens up. Place in the refrigerator while the cream puffs are baking and cooling. Once the cream puffs are cooled, remove pudding from the refrigerator and gently fold in 1 cup of cool whip.

4. Cut a slit in each cream puff and fill with the pudding mixture, or cool whip. Lightly dust with some powdered sugar. Serve and enjoy!

CLASSIC SOUTHERN CHESS PIE

INGREDIENTS:

- 1 Stick Butter (melted then cooled)
- 2 Cups Granulated White Sugar
- 1 Tsp. Vanilla
- 4 Eggs (lightly beaten)
- 1 Tbsp. All-Purpose Flour
- 2 Tbsp. Yellow Corn Meal (fine ground)
- ¼ Tsp. Salt
- 1 Tbsp. White Vinegar
- ¼ Cup Evaporated Milk
- 1 9-inch Ready to Bake Pie Crust
- Garnish with Whipping Cream

Prep. time:
10 min

Total time:
75 min

Serves: 5

DIRECTIONS:

1. Preheat oven to 425 degrees.
2. In a mixing bowl, add the cooled melted butter, granulated white sugar, and vanilla. Mix together with an electric hand mixer. Pour in the eggs and mix together until blended. Then add the flour, cornmeal, salt, white vinegar, and evaporated milk. Mix together until well combined.
3. Pour the filling into a 9-inch unbaked pie crust, and fill ¼-inch from the top.
4. Place the pie on the lowest rack in the oven and bake at 425 degrees for 10 minutes. Then reduce heat to 300 degrees, and bake for 45 to 55, or until golden brown around the edges, and the center of the pie jiggles a little bit. Turn the oven off and let the pie cool in the oven.
5. Serve warm, or chilled, top with whipping cream and enjoy this classic delicious pie!

BUTTER PECAN CHEESECAKE

INGREDIENTS:

- 2 8oz. Packages Cream Cheese (softened)
- 1 Cup Granulated White Sugar
- 3 Tbsp. Sour Cream
- 2 Eggs (lightly beaten)
- 2 Tbsp. Butter Flavoring
- 1 Tsp. Vanilla
- ¾ Cups Chopped Pecans
- 1 Ready to Use 10-inch Graham Cracker Crusts

Toppings:
- Chopped Pecans, Caramel Sauce, Whipping Cream

Prep. time:
10 min

Total time:
70 min

Serves: 5-6

DIRECTIONS:

1. Preheat oven to 300 degrees.

2. In a mixing bowl, add the softened cream cheese, granulated white sugar, and sour cream. Blend together using an electric hand mixer for about 1 minute. Add eggs, butter flavoring, and vanilla, and blend together for about 4 minutes. Then fold in the chopped pecans.

3. Pour the filling into the ready to use graham cracker crust.

4. Place in the oven and bake at 300 degrees for 65 to 70 minutes, or until golden brown around the outside edge of the filling. Remove from the oven, place on a wire rack and let cool. Then place in the refrigerator for several hours.

5. Serve and sprinkle with chopped pecans, drizzle with caramel sauce, and a dollop of whipping cream and enjoy!

ICELANDIC KLEINURS DEEP FRIED DOUGHNUTS

INGREDIENTS:

- ½ Cup Buttermilk
- 1 Tsp. Baking Soda
- ½ Cup Sour Cream
- 1 Cup Whole Milk
- 1 Tsp. Vanilla
- 4 Eggs
- 2½ Tsp. Baking Powder
- 1 Tsp. Salt
- 2½ Tsp. Ground Cardamom
- 4 Cups Granulated White Sugar
- 5 Lbs. All-Purpose Flour
- 4 Cups Lard
- 4 Cups All-Vegetable Shortening

Prep. time:
15 min

Total time:
60 min

Serves: 10

DIRECTIONS:

1. In a small bowl, stir together buttermilk and baking soda. Once it starts to foam, stir in sour cream, then pour into a stand mixer. Use a paddle attachment and set the mixer on low speed. Add whole milk, vanilla, and eggs and blend together.

2. Continue mixing on low speed and add about 1 cup of flour. Then add baking powder, salt, cardamom and sugar. Slowly start adding in flour and mix until the dough is soft and not sticky.

3. Divide the dough into 4 equal parts and form into balls. Take one of the dough balls and place on a floured surface. Dust with a little flour and roll it out to about ¼-inch thick. Using a pastry rotary cutter, cut the dough into long strips, then cut the opposite way to form a diamond shape. Make a slit in the center of each diamond shape. Then take one end and pull it through the slit so it will form into a knot. Repeat the process with the remaining dough.

4. Heat lard and vegetable shortening to 375 degrees in a large pot (clip a thermometer to the pot and measure temperature when adding new dough knots into the pot). Gently drop the dough knots into the pot (fry in small batches so the pot isn't overcrowded) and fry until one side is golden brown, then turn each one over and fry the other side until golden brown. Remove the Kleinur from the oil and set aside on a baking sheet lined with paper towels to drain and cool. These are so delicious, they are crispy on the outside and tender on the inside and just perfect for dunking in coffee!

MAMA'S CHOCOLATE MERINGUE PIE

INGREDIENTS:
- 1 Ready to Bake Pie Crust

Pie Filling:
- 1 Cup Granulated White Sugar
- 4 Tbsp. Unsweetened Cocoa Powder
- 4 Tbsp. Self-Rising Flour
- ¼ Tsp. Salt
- 2 Egg Yolks
- 2 Cups Milk
- 1 Tsp. Vanilla
- ½ Stick Butter

Meringue:
- 4 Egg Whites
- ¼ Cup Granulated White Sugar
- ¼ Tsp. Cream of Tartar
- 1 Tsp. Vanilla

Chocolate Shavings

Prep. time:
30 min

Total time:
4 hours

Serves: 10

Mama Marge
&
Miss Sheila

DIRECTIONS:

1. Bring the pie crust to room temperature before baking. Then prick the bottom of the crust with a fork. Preheat the oven to 400 degrees. Bake the pie crust for 10 to 12 minutes, or until light golden brown. Remove it from the oven, place on a wire rack and let it cool.

2. Make the Pie Filling: In a microwave-safe bowl, whisk together the white sugar, cocoa powder, self-rising flour, and salt. Pour in about ½ cup of the milk and whisk until combined. Then add the egg yolks and stir until well blended. Slowly pour in the remaining milk and stir until the pie filling is smooth, then add the butter.

3. Place in the microwave and cook for 5 to 6 minutes, stirring every couple of minutes until the pie filling has thickened and is a pudding consistency. Remove from the microwave and add the vanilla. Then pour it into the baked pie crust.

4. Make the Meringue: In a bowl, add the egg whites, and beat them with an electric hand mixer on high speed until they form soft peaks. Then turn the speed down to low and add the sugar, cream of tartar, and vanilla and beat until the egg whites form stiff peaks.

5. Gently spoon the meringue on top of the pie filling and spread it to the edge of the pie crust. Place the pie in a preheated oven and bake at 400 degrees for 3 to 4 minutes, or until the meringue turns golden brown. Remove from the oven and let it cook on a wire rack, then place in the refrigerator to chill for about 2 to 4 hours.

6. Garnish with chocolate shavings and serve and enjoy this incredibly delicious chocolate pie!

PUMPKIN CREAM CHEESE MUFFINS

INGREDIENTS:

Cream Cheese Filling:

- 1 8oz. Package Cream Cheese (room temperature)
- ⅓ Cup Granulated White Sugar
- 1 Large Egg (room temperature)
- ½ Tsp. Pure Vanilla Extract

Pumpkin Muffins:

- 1½ Cups All-Purpose Flour
- 1 Cup Granulated White Sugar
- 1 Tsp. Baking Powder
- ½ Tsp. Baking Soda
- 1 Tsp. Ground Cinnamon
- 1 Tsp. Pumpkin Pie Spice
- ½ Tsp. Salt
- 1 Stick Butter (softened)
- 2 Large Eggs (room temperature)
- 1 Tsp. Pure Vanilla Extract
- ¾ Cup 100% Pure Canned Pumpkin

Prep. time:
10 min

Total time:
35 min

Serves: 6

DIRECTIONS:

1. Preheat oven to 350 degrees. Spray a 12-cup muffin pan with nonstick cooking spray.

2. Cream Cheese Filling: In a bowl, add the cream cheese and beat with an electric hand mixer until creamy and smooth. Then add the sugar, egg, and vanilla extract, and beat until blended, smooth and creamy. Set aside while preparing the muffins.

3. Pumpkin Muffins: In a bowl, add the flour, sugar, baking powder, baking soda, cinnamon, pumpkin pie spice, and salt and whisk together well. Then add the butter, eggs, vanilla extract, and canned pumpkin, and beat together with the hand mixer on medium speed for about 1 minute, or until the batter is smooth.

4. Fill each muffin cup evenly (about ⅔ full) with the pumpkin batter using an ice cream scoop, or spoon. Using a spoon, make a well in the center of the batter of each muffin and then add the cream cheese filling into the well using an ice cream scoop, or spoon.

5. Place on the center rack in the oven and bake for about 18 to 20 minutes, or until the cream cheese filling has set, and the pumpkin muffin feels springy to the touch, and a toothpick inserted into the pumpkin muffin comes out clean. Place on a wire rack to cool.